Power, Politics, and the Leadership Landscape

Navigating Modern Organizations

Second Edition 2025

Dr. Eileen Griffin-Ray

With thanks to all the amazing leaders and colleagues I have had the opportunity to work with and learn from.

Power, Politics and the Leadership Landscape
Navigating Modern Organizations

Copyright © 2023/2025 Eileen Griffin-Ray
All rights reserved.
ISBN-13:9798374823769

No part of this publication may be reproduced, stored in a retrieval system, or transmitted in any form or by any means, electronic, mechanical, photocopying, recording, scanning, or otherwise, except as permitted under Section 107 or 108 of the 1976 United States Copyright Act, without either the prior written permission of the publisher or author.

Power, Politics, and the Leadership Landscape/Dr. Eileen Griffin-Ray

Printed in the United States of America

TABLE OF CONTENTS

Preface   1

1. INTRODUCTION   3
2. DECISION-MAKING   10
3. POWER AND CONTROL   26
4. POWER AND DECISIONS   55
5. LEADERS, FOLLOWERS AND STRUCTURE   69
6. AUTHENTIC AND ADAPTIVE LEADERS   84
7. PURPOSE, ETHICS, AND INTENTION   107
8. TRAINING LEADERS   127
9. SUCCESSFULLY NAVIGATING   157

Appendix A   171

References   174

PREFACE

This book was written for the many people struggling with organizational issues. The modern organization is challenging and often incredibly fast-paced. Technology has made modern organizations even more complicated and employees who continue to learn and grow are likely to be more valued than those who do not invest in their own career.

There is a great deal to know about any role before one begins a new job. People are often thrust into roles before they are prepared, or roles they are never suited for. This can undermine the entire organization and damage the morale of staff. This book includes both philosophical background and practical application for a better understanding of organizational structure and leadership. We address how employees can learn to be better followers while positioning themselves to eventually become successful leaders. The role of power and influence in politics and business is addressed. How power is used and how decisions are made are important aspects of a professional life. Developing a better understanding, and more skilled application of these tools may be very useful for people at all levels of an organization.

The importance of purpose and intention are critical aspects, not only of success, but for personal happiness in life. A fulfilling job, an honorable purpose, and intentionally living ethically can make the workplace a positive and healthy environment. This book will cover ethics, purpose, and how to recognize a healthy work environment. We will cover training and how and when to develop employees for advancement and leadership.

Interviews were conducted with several leaders with many years of experience. Personal stories and lessons learned shared by people with many years of professional experience illustrate real people facing real situations and how they were handled. With the benefit of hindsight those providing content for this book can share their success, but also what they learned from any failures they may have experienced. Written to provide guidance to the individual, as well as the organization, this can be used as a training tool or a basis for discussion between leader and follower. It can be a source for teams looking to build leaders and board members seeking succession planning guidance. It can be for an individual interested in improving his or her understanding of the leadership landscape. I hope many people find this information valuable and useful.

CHAPTER ONE
INTRODUCTION

Many books have been written over the years attempting to guide people through the complex organizational world. There is much more to organizational life than most people realize when they first enter the labor market. While we may muddle through our first job, we eventually pick up tools and techniques to help make us a better contributor and, potentially, set us up on the path towards leadership. Most of us can remember the first day at our first job. The fear, anticipation, excitement, and curiosity of that experience can impact each future role we take and organization we join. We strive for acceptance, appreciation, and ultimately success. We want to feel like our days are purposeful and our activities impactful. The landscape is full of opportunities. We just need to know how to work through the terrain, recognizing the harmful weeds and poison berries, so we can walk down a peaceful path and find the pot of gold, or the watch of gold, at the end of the employment rainbow.

Leadership is an ideal and most people can envision what they perceive a great leader to be. While we believe we can recognize good leaders, we don't always know how to function as good leaders. It is not as easy as pop culture and consultants make it sound. Learning to lead anything takes several skills, traits, abilities, attitudes, and techniques.

One of the best ways to learn to improve in any area is to ask experts. With the benefit of years of experience, those senior to us can help us learn by sharing their history. Anyone interested in improving would be wise to listen to other people with specific, relevant knowledge and a proven track record of success. Too many organizations perpetuate poor organizational leadership by promoting people lacking in capabilities and then allowing those people to train and mentor new employees. It is no mystery why organizations become mired in operational inefficiency and antiquity. Without strong leaders looking at efficiencies and opportunities for improvement, an organization will stagnate. Without people within the organizational hierarchy willing to question policies and processes and without an environment that fosters discussion and debate an organization will decline and the individuals will suffer. Given the importance of recruiting, retaining, and developing employees, one would think the process would take high priority in most organizations, yet it does not. Many organizations continue to neglect the importance of identifying, developing, and nurturing future leaders.

Recently, a colleague told me about a situation at her organization. Due to consolidation, two departments were merged into one. Both departments had a manager. When the decision was made to have only one department with this function, it meant they would only need one manager. This resulted in two managers competing for the same role. In the new role, the manager would now oversee a much larger function and would be expected to be promoted to a higher level in a very short period of time. This decision, between the two, would result in one person staying with the organization, positioned for leadership, and the other person losing their job entirely. Some people in the organization familiar with the situation assumed it would the person we will call "Alex" and were very surprised when the selection was made resulting in the retention of person we will call "Bill". Some department heads and other leaders questioned the choice. My colleague said when questioned, the response from upper management was that while Alex was certainly a better leader than Bill, he was not as knowledgeable on the operational functions of the job. They chose the person who had better operational knowledge of the job rather than the person with leadership skills.

If this is an accurate explanation for the selection, this was probably a significant mistake. It is much easier to train functionality than it is to develop leaders. They planned to promote Bill to a leadership role, yet they know leadership is his weakness. Alex was weaker on the operational aspects of the role but had the leadership skills the new role would require. As the role was expected to continue to grow the operational pieces would become far less important. More of the operations would be delegated as the role evolved into a leadership position. Why would they choose the person who was not likely to be a successful leader?

Scenarios like this are not unusual. Part of the dissonance between wanting a good leader and having a good leader is that many in powerful positions don't really want other people who can lead. If you are allowing people to lead and you have more than one good leader in an organization, you will have disagreement. Naturally, a good leader, a decisive leader, will often state their position, share their opinion, and weigh in on decisions, even when it is in opposition to another leader. In a healthy environment, this debate can be an enormous benefit to an organization.

Various ideas, theories, experiences, and diversity of opinions and perspectives can enhance discussion and provide options, alternatives, and improvements. If done correctly, with informed opinions, discussions can be rich with various viewpoints. For many, however, confrontation is uncomfortable. The perception of disagreement is that it is antagonistic. Debate is considered disrespectful. A CEO or top leader may feel threatened by another individual who is simply seeking the best solution for the organization. A top leader may not want his or her authority challenged. Unfortunately, a different opinion may be perceived as confrontational. Anyone confronting the powerful may be sidelined from future discussions either organizationally or emotionally by making sure they feel that their involvement is not appreciated or expected.

True leaders tend to be willing to disagree and engage in difficult conversations. If that is perceived as unpleasant, it is easy to see why some in upper management actually reject upcoming leaders, or discourage them from upward mobility, as their potential encroaches upon a senior leader's ultimate authority. For this reason, organizations often discount or discourage those who could become their best leaders. It may be unintended or accidental. It could be just lack of knowledge. It could be that the emotional discomfort of a person perceived as confrontational clouds the strategic objective of developing and advancing leaders.

If we try to listen to other people and really hear them, we may find that they are not confrontational at all. Healthy debate can be invaluable and should be encouraged in a forward thinking, growth-oriented organization. It can be done respectfully, civilly, and positively. This is an area where many leadership teams need improvement.

Perhaps the most important aspect of leadership is decision-making. We will cover decisions, the process of decision-making, and the role of the decision maker extensively. The other component I consider essential to leadership is ethics. Without a positive foundational framework, a leader will not have the character to seek solutions for the betterment of others when it is detrimental to himself or herself. While the current culture strives to remove any aspect of religion, faith or even the existence of God from organizations, including the workplace and classrooms, evidence mounts of the foolishness of that effort. As organizations become more secular, they become less introspective and less committed to the good, as opposed to the profitable or the expedient. Quality leaders will display good judgment and be skilled deciders and they will function within an ethical framework.

In this book we will cover topics of leadership, decision-making, the role of power and influence, and development of human capital. Historical theories and ideas are included as well as original interviews of leaders with many years of experience. Leaders with real experience share their stories and advice for those seeking advancement or improved skills. Four leaders with many years of management background were interviewed and asked to provide answers to several open-ended questions. Each of these leaders contributed their lived experiences and knowledge for the benefit of the reader. Each of these leaders shared their advice, guidance, and lessons learned from their own past. Brief biographies of each participant are included in Appendix A.

We will describe decision-making processes and strategies for better decision-making and skill improvement. We will cover training and what seems to be lacking in current leadership development programs. This book should generate ideas and thought-provoking questions for reflection and consideration. The goal of this book is advancement of skills and thoughts for any individual interested in understanding and improving leadership skills. It will hopefully be helpful to those aspiring towards leadership or a larger role in the decision making of their organization. Conversations that have previously were avoided, or never even considered, may need to take place to begin the process of establishing a better organizational culture. It may take a subordinate to push a leader to engage in conversation and to be interested in the contributions of other team members in decision-making. Improvements may come from the bottom to the top in the hierarchy, rather than the other way around. These conversations need to take place for organizations to seriously start building leadership capabilities. Those seeking leadership roles have a vested interest in making sure that their organization is interested in having leaders and developing leaders. If your current organization seems to suppress ideas, discourage honest discussion and debate, it may be that the organizational culture is not conducive to a successful long-term career. The hope is this book will provide food for thought as well as actual steps that will improve the organizational lives of those living within the leadership landscape.

CHAPTER TWO
DECISIONS AND DECISION-MAKING

When you take the lead, you grab the reins and begin driving a team towards a goal or through a mission. Twists and turns, fraught with risk and uncertainty, require judgement, discernment, and decision-making ability. Making good decisions with reliable information and thoughtfulness are critical components of leadership. You also need to know what you believe before you can make decisions and lead teams. What framework do you use to make your decisions and guide your followers?

We expect leaders to make good decisions, not just for themselves, but for the groups they are leading. Participant Mark pointed out the importance of consensus building for leaders. He said you need to build support and develop relationships throughout the organization and to external partners.

> One of the things I always point to is consensus buildings. I think a leader really has to have that skill of being able to build a consensus around the vision. Again, it goes back to the vision because if you can't get your people to buy in then and follow then you are probably going to have a problem. It's probably not the right role for a person to not be good at building consensus. If you can't build consensus and I think that creates a different

kind of challenge. I think to be a good consensus builder. (M.H. 2020)

We expect anyone in leadership to be skilled in the art of decision-making, knowing when to build consensus, when to be authoritative and when to be inclusive, but many are not. There is an obvious gap between the expectations of leaders and the actual performance of leaders. Why is that? Why is there so much disappointment in leaders today and the decisions they are making? What if more leaders made a determined effort to improve their decision-making skills?

> Making decisions is something humans do constantly while they are conscious, and how we do that has been studied in many disciplines. In short, if humans could improve their individual and collective decision-making they could improve their well-being (Chandler & Kirsch, 2018 p. 87).

In leadership, skilled decision-making can have significant impact. Employees, partners, clients, customers, and various other stakeholders can be affected positively or negatively by a leader's decision. The decision of an individual or group of leaders may have profound implications beyond the immediate into an extended future period of time. One decision can create a career. One decision can destroy a career. One decision can motivate an entire organization. One decision can demoralize an entire organization. The ability leaders have to apply an effective decision-making process determines the direction of the organization. Each individual that is part of the organization will move with the organization, at least as long as they choose to remain within the organization.

Jack Welch led General Electric to great success during his forty-year career. As the CEO he became known as an outstanding leader, often asked to share his wisdom and secrets for success. In his book, Winning, he explained some of his policies and practices. His focus was on people, teamwork, and profits in a very competitive environment (Welsch, 2005). While Welsch (2005) shared his knowledge and strategies for success, he also acknowledged that there is no one road to becoming a leadership legend. Leaders come in varieties with different styles and organizational rules; however, he said, there are some ways of leading that seem to result in universal success. One of his eight rules of leading addresses decision-making.

"Leaders have the courage to make unpopular decisions and gut calls" (Welch, 2005, p. 63). Welch defines "gut" as those instincts that don't fit into a metric, quantitative formula, or any technical rationale. There is an instinct about a decision and sometimes it is just intuition that comes from years of experience. Seasoned leaders often sense what others may take hours or weeks to research. "Leaders are faced with gut calls all the time" (Welch, 2005, p. 73). When making decisions, it is not always possible to have as much information as you may like. Leaders often hesitate in making a decision pending additional data or research. Sometimes the time lost in this process hampers the ability for an organization to be competitive. Sometimes it is not possible to find data to support a decision, or it is just not realistic to rely on data. A metrics-driven or quantitative solution may leave gaps or holes in relevant considerations. Seasoned leaders will have to rely on the instinct they have honed over time to make a decision, whether or not they are able to gather every relevant piece of information.

In our current culture, leaders like Welch might face criticism for being too direct or too confrontational. Some of the best organizations are led by those, like Welch, who can make unilateral decisions without always taking the time to solicit input. Leaders may need to do what they believe is best and work through the public relations issues later.

Successful leaders are often referred to as, "decisive" and "determined". Those qualities are consistently referenced as laudable for leaders in business, politics, and any type of organization. Clear and decisive answers define a great leader, according to former Prime Minister Margaret Thatcher. This does not include compromise or capitulation. "Throughout my political life, I have usually sought to avoid compromise, because it more often than not turns out to involve an abdication of principle. In international affairs, it is often also symptomatic of muddle and weakness" (Thatcher, 2002, p. 243).

Decision-making should not be fraught with weakness and uncertainty. Trying to please all involved rarely, if ever, works and compromise, as Thatcher suggests, may result in a decision that is not optimal, but simply less offensive or more tolerable to a wide range of differing opinions. It may be that compromise would lead to a path in conflict with principles or values. A leader needs to know what he or she believes to know when compromise is untenable. A violation of principles or values should not be acceptable to an ethical leader. Followers can more easily follow when consistent values are in evidence.

> Because leadership affects many lives, the concept we use must be spacious. It has to allow for the values of various cultures and organizations. It cannot be imperialistic. Yet we cannot beg the issue altogether by saying that leadership is value-free and define it simply in terms of its instruments (influence, formal powers, prominence) or personal resources (skills, bearing, temperament). Those who listen to us do more with what we say. They turn instruments and resources into values that orient their professional life (Heifetz, 1994, p. 26).

Leadership, or lack thereof, can have an impact far beyond the individual leader and his or her team. Even without realizing it, you may be impacting the values of the people below you or around you in an organization. Culture has an enormous impact on organizations. While leaders should consider individual culture and diversity of staff, it is also incumbent upon individuals to recognize organizational culture where they work. Organizational culture can be deeply rooted and embedded. It is far easier to find an organization where there is a cultural fit than it is to change organizational culture.

Many leaders fail to recognize the influence they have on subordinates or constituents. They don't even realize when followers are listening and appreciate what they are hearing. They may not be aware of the behavior and practices that they are modeling while in the presence of other staff members. Often, busy leaders function in their own world and, for many reasons, disconnect from the community. It may be a simple lack of awareness, or a deeper problem of disassociation. In politics, it is often noted how those remaining in Washington, D.C. for an extended period of time become disconnected from those they supposedly represent. Those at the highest levels of power in the nation live in a world most of us cannot even fathom. When Americans in small towns and neighborhoods across the country struggle with rising gas prices or food prices, many in Washington cannot relate at all. They have not had to consider life under a tight budget, at least not for many years. Some may not understand how a family must restrict activities just to stay afloat month to month. Leading people requires relating to people. This means getting "off the balcony" and integrating with those you lead (Northouse, 2016). Leaders should not be disconnected or isolated from their followers, constituents, or community or organizational members.

While there are certainly differences in what one believes a good leader is, there also tends to be broad agreement on specific characteristics. Most organizational participants immediately cite honesty and integrity when describing a good leader and someone they would like to work for. When decisions are made organizationally the rationale for the decision can often be very clear. While all employees may not be told of the discussion, the debate, or the issues involved, they should not often be surprised by a result if the leader or leaders are consistent and reliable. Good leaders consistently make principled decisions; those based on moral judgement or with ethical considerations. The decision-making process is thoughtful, serious, sensitive, and informed. Foresight, vision, and a macro-level approach means more than just reactionary conclusions.

> In the leadership literature, many scholars usually agree on what constitutes the qualities of a good leader. Some of these qualities, among others, include a clear sense of purpose and direction or vision, persistence, strong self-image, the craving for relevant knowledge and education, a love of what they do and to do what they love, ability to energize and attract others, emotional maturity, caring, commitment, integrity, responsibility, accountability, ability to listen, accessibility, optimism, honestly, trustworthiness, motivation, enthusiasm, excellent followers, and many others (Adjibolosoo, 2018, p. 102).

It is much easier to follow a leader when one believes they are honest and trustworthy. It is more satisfying and fulfilling to follow someone who is working towards the good, and not the selfish end. Leaders generate followers when they are viewed as honest, loyal, and committed to the task and team. Legendary coach, John Wooden, identified reasons for leadership success.

> I'm convinced that regardless of the task, leaders must be enthusiastic and really enjoy what they're doing if they expect those under their supervision to work near their respective levels

of competency. With few exceptions, an unenthusiastic leader will keep those under his or her charge from achieving their collective best (Wooden, 2005, p. 35).

For anyone thinking they would like to be in leadership, I would first suggest an honest self-assessment and a reality check on what a leader really is. Before accepting a leadership position, it's helpful to understand what the role entails, and the significance of decisions made by leaders. If you are thinking to yourself, "well, that seems obvious" let me assure you that many people fail to consider the difficulties focusing only on the benefits. I have known many people in leadership roles in my career, but I have encountered few actual leaders.

There are typical qualities, attributes, and skills normally associated with a good leader. Decision-making is always associated with leadership. If one is considered a failed leader, it is often due to decisions made or the decisions not made. Those refusing to make decisions create a culture of non-decision, with deep and lasting consequences (Griffin-Ray, 2022). Not making a decision, a history of avoiding or deflecting decisions, or making poor decisions will define a leader. In some cases, depending on the level of risk, just one really bad decision may define an individual in terms of overall leadership. This is true in almost any environment from business to non-profits to government and politics.

When I asked the group of leaders I interviewed about decision-making, there was a strong defense of the need for good judgment and the ability to make good decisions. All the participants agreed that decision making was key to leadership. Some said it was the most important thing for anyone in a management or leadership position. Participant Harold said, "Decision making is very important for management. It is vital to make good decisions both for yourself and the organization" (H.G. 2022).

Participant Mel concurred and elaborated on the type of decider one needs to be in order to be successful in a leadership or management role.
> It's one of the most critical parts or attributes of management. You have to have people in leadership who can make those decisions. They have to be people who are not afraid to make tough decisions. You can't be a leader if you can't make tough decisions or if you are in the middle of the road. Especially if other people depend on you. If others are depending on you to make decisions you have to make them – good, bad, or indifferent, (M.C., 2022).

Another participant with decades of experience in leadership, Mark, said that decision-making is one of the most important things leaders learn, yet it is also one of the last things they learn. He explained that it is something not often focused on for new managers, so new managers make many mistakes. Learning from those mistakes is key. "I made a lot of mistakes in the beginning. When you are a younger manager and newer manager you don't have a lot of experience to go off your gut. You rely a lot on instinct" (M.H., 2022).

Participant Steve said that decision making is essential for every level of the organization. He explained how challenging it is to determine the process for decision-making when there are multiple layers and numerous projects happening at the same time. With that level of complexity, one leader could not possibly be effective with a centralized decision-making process. "With about 75 people making decisions each week on a project – that could be 600-900 decisions being made a week. There's no way that I can scale myself to oversee that" (S. S., 2022). Steve determined the best way to handle that number of decisions is to de-centralize and ensure that other staff members have the ability and authority to make decisions.

> The key part of my role (in decision-making) was to help people make the best decisions they can at the time and when they make bad decisions, help them make better decisions the next time. I've viewed that as a measure of my success, to the degree that I engage with younger staff, those early career staff, to really help nurture them through those early steps of the process and to try to shape more senior staff who need shaping. (S.S., 2022)

Steve described this approach as a universal concept regardless of where you work, what kind of organization, or who you are, and decision-making is always important. "You are going to have to make decisions every day, and you want people to make the best decisions possible" (S.S., 2022).

Since they all agreed on the importance of decision-making, I asked how they typically made decisions. What was their process or their plan when faced with a difficult decision? What were some of the most important decisions they had made? The Participants all explained that sometimes they needed to rely on the expertise of others, or the knowledge and access of people more directly involved. Sometimes, they made the decision unilaterally, trusting their own judgment and expertise. Participant Harold acknowledged that in his personal life all of his decisions were made in cooperation with his wife, but his decision-making process at work did not always include any other person. "In business I made some decisions on my own and some together as a group" (H.G., 2022).

Mel said that his decision-making process evolved over time, and it changed depending on the situation and the group or groups involved. As a leader with layers of managers and teams below him, there was a level of complexity in the structure that necessarily impacted the decision-making process.

> Eventually I got to where (decision-making) was more of a combination. With the leadership team – people that reported directly to me – they had different insights because they were closer to the day-to-day operations. There was also a benefit to getting them involved earlier as it made them feel more part of the decision and more supportive. Initially I was someone who mostly made decisions independently. I evolved over time. I realized that I had not collected enough data – did not have

> enough intel to make that decision. I learned that I needed to ask more questions, get more details, involve more people. I was not afraid to make a decision, but I decided I needed to get more input to make a good decision. (M.C., 2022)

Sometimes, unliteral decision-making is the best method. "There are those decisions where you have to make the call because you're the trusted leaders" (M.H., 2022). As a trusted leader, and one with a strong and reliable moral compass, followers will expect and appreciate someone who takes control particularly in a difficult or uncomfortable situation. A leader who portrays ambiguity risks the loss of loyal followers. "In the later part of my career, I would rely on past experiences. A decision would be something I faced before" (M.C., 2022).

> Once you have, or you believe you have, more experience you are going to make that decision having thought it through. Maybe having dealt with it before. You have made that type of decision before, or you know you have the knowledge from previous experience. At some point it's that decision making process we have already worked through. You know what it takes to make it work. (M.H. 2022)

Some types of decisions require more strategic thought in how they are made. Many busy leaders run at such a pace that they do not often have the luxury of time to make a strategic plan for a thoughtful decision. The most important decisions should be handled differently than those of less significance. "The most important decisions managers make is deciding who to hire," (H.G, 2022). Harold emphasized the significance of a hiring decision over other types of decisions that must be made. "The most important decision making is hiring. You are either a beneficiary or a victim of the people you hire." (H.G. 2022)

Steve said that sometimes he made decisions unilaterally and sometimes he involved a group depending on the situation. "It becomes more critical when the breadth or the repercussions of the decision are broader. If it's within the domain of my day job responsibility, I would feel very comfortable making a decision that relates to me. But if it has broader application, either in our organization or in other organizations I might include others in that process" (S.S., 2022).

Mel said he developed an ordered process for making decisions. "I go to the worst-case scenario and work backwards when I make a decision," (M.C., 2022). "I eliminate everything that can possibly go wrong and work my way back. How many people will be affected? How does it affect others and how many people will benefit? I gather as much information as I can and as early as I can. I get all the facts and talk to all the people involved" (M.C., 2022).

Steve described his decision-making process as based on both training and experience, as well as outcomes. "I am frequently looking for the best outcome for as broad an audience as possible" (S.S., 2022). He also addressed the time element of decision-making. He explained that some managers, particularly those newer in management, think they need to make decisions quicker than they really need to or they can feel pressured to make a quick decision to prove that they are decisive and up to the task of leadership. "There's probably more room to consult with others to make the decision, and make the best decision possible" (S.S., 2022).

In a recent *National Review* article Richard Brookehiser (2021), described what he considered a leadership failure based on decision-making. Brookehiser (2021) wrote that he thought the U.S. President who made the worst decisions during wartime was probably President James Madison during the Chesapeake theater in 1814. As the British landed and began their movement northward, Madison was faced with several decisions. "At this moment of peril Madison stuck with a secretary of war – John Armstrong – who was no longer consulting him, and a commander in the field – William Winder – whom he had appointed for political reasons (Winder's uncle was governor of Maryland at the time)." Madison had people in key positions who were not following the directions provided by the person in the top leadership role. Armstrong made his own decisions. He decided against defending Washington D.C. believing there would be no conflict reaching that part of the country. Winder, while generating a great deal of activity, accomplished nothing. All the effort he engaged in, "amounted to nothing because he was in over his head" (Brookehiser, 2022). Winder created a lot of commotion but hid behind a cloud of a non-decision. As for President Madison, he was unable to correctly address the failings of his two key subordinates. The President's reaction to the decisions and non-decisions of these two men was simply, "passive aggressive suggestions that they do better" (Brookehiser, 2021).

 A leader afraid to redirect his or her own staff will perpetuate poor decisions and allow negative consequences and bad outcomes. Leaders must have courage and fortitude and the ability to confront any individual or situation that needs correction. Those who prefer popularity and who shy away from direct discussions, often involving uncomfortable confrontations, are not those typically suited to leadership roles. There are many excellent opportunities for those who desire to be liked, but leadership is not one of them. A leader may be popular, but he or she cannot fear making decisions or dealing with problems in service to maintaining popularity. "The best manager I ever worked for was a person who knew all the answers to the questions before he asked you," Participant Mel said. "He was very intelligent. He did a lot of research, collected data, and his proposal would not have a single mistake. He was meticulous. He would make tough decisions, and they were not always favorable, but he did it," (M.C., 2022).

 Another issue raised in Brookehiser's review of President Madison's decisions is the problem with personal relationships and favoritism in leadership. If a leader promotes a person for his or her own benefit, there is an inherent payback expectation. Favoritism can destroy a team as one person is treated differently than others. The inherent unfairness of disparate treatment will turn employees against their leader. Many companies avoid allowing family members to work together due to favoritism or any other issue related to personal connections. Certainly, family members should never be in a position where one family member reports to another. This is bound to cause problems. One of the top reasons employees become frustrated with their job is their manager's bias or unfair treatment, real or perceived. Decisions that may adversely affect the person you "owe" will probably be infused with bias. While one employee's concerns can be quickly dismissed, the favored employee's concerns may become front and center of an organizational decision.

Leaders without a strong moral compass, when faced with these situations, will likely fail. Leaders guided by ethical principles are far more likely to strive to be fair and reasonable with employees and to be consistent and clear in their decision-making. We will talk further about ethics and character later in a later chapter, but next we are going to cover the role of power.

CHAPTER THREE
POWER AND CONTROL

It seems like a daily occurrence that we hear about some abuse of power and control or corruption in organizations once respected and admired. There are many sordid tales of companies, once admired, becoming disgraced. Names like Enron, Arthur Anderson, KPMG, Kraft Heinz, and Wells Fargo have all been tainted by scandal. Both business and government seem to be suffering from a more significant affliction of corruption than in the past. Questions have been raised about the integrity of the Federal Bureau of Investigation (FBI). As the COVID-19 pandemic dragged on, many Americans questioned the veracity of the Center for Disease Control (CDC). Some Governors were afforded unilateral authority under emergency declarations due to the pandemic and when the time came to return that power, some clung tightly to the authoritarian control (Fillmore, 2022). In some states, the power-hungry had to be reminded by the legislature that tyranny will not be tolerated. Government and business, governors, and CEOs, find landmines along the landscape of power. It would appear that those in power seem to only crave more power and, in some cases, be willing to do almost anything to retain power once acquired.

Sen (2009) writes extensively about the corrupting influence of power. He states that the best solution to combat corruptive power is democracy. In a free society we have "countervailing power" which should restrain the corrupt leader (p. 81). Sen (2009) notices, however, how things have changed in the United States in recent years as the executive branch has extended power beyond what was intended in the constitution, and this allows for the infestation of corruption. A democracy contains intended checks and balances. When one branch, division, section, or even individual of the government acquires more power than is intended, the delicate dance of democracy is imperiled.

The American founding fathers understood that power corrupts, and unilateral authority would only lead to misery for the people. They designed a government with checks and balances and specifically assigned authority to keep the power hungry from imposing tyranny. Each part of the system is designed to protect against tyranny from another part of the system. Organizations, like governments, should establish a system of authority with guardrails and protections throughout the structure to prevent abuse of power and corruption. A brilliantly crafted balance of power with a focus on ethical leadership, values, character, and morality can ensure a positive, healthy, culture for most organizations.

Corruption

Leadership is a great responsibility and those in positions of power must recognize it as a responsibility, not just a right to authority. There is a responsibility to the organization, and to each person assigned within the hierarchy. A person should not be in a position of leadership solely to enrich himself or herself, but to improve the lives of those he or she leads and to achieve the goals, projects, or tasks assigned. The role may be defined clearly, yet as soon as a person gains a position of power, often corruption creeps into the leadership landscape. Often people drawn to leadership roles are those craving power, rather than those driven by integrity.

Politics seems to draw the type of people who crave power and authority. People often are dismayed at the choices they have when going to vote for elected leaders. Politicians are expected to serve their constituents, yet many of them seem focused on serving themselves. Many policies are created, and decisions are made, by people in these leadership roles from the President all the way down to local city councils and school boards. Each person serving in one of these roles in setting direction and leading their respective constituency. Currently, Congress has a very low approval rating because many people simply don't trust them. They believe many in power hold on to power too long and use it for the wrong reasons.

There may be something about power that makes people feel that they can engage in any behavior they choose without consequence. At the highest level of authority arrogance may infiltrate the psyche and the leader no longer believes the rules apply to him or her. The person who makes the rules, like those elected to the legislature, may believe that they are exempt from the rules. During the pandemic, many leaders dictated rules for "the people" yet they were caught ignoring the rules themselves.

Many women in my community suddenly started to go gray when hairdressers were shut down, yet Nancy Pelosi never saw a single gray hair. She was caught on camera having her hair done while the rest of America learned to adapt.

People across the country craved social time and an evening out at a good restaurant. California was one of the states with the tightest restrictions. Californians could not even go to the beach due to the rules dictated by Governor Gavin Newsom. Californians were not happy when Newsom was caught attending a social dinner with a group of friends at an upscale restaurant. Elderly people were not even allowed to have family members over for a birthday party. The Governor, however, could go to a restaurant without fear of consequences.

Lower-level leaders should be able to trust upper-level management. We need to trust the person we report to and see that individual as a source of advice and development. For a multitude of reasons, including career pathing, succession planning, and the success of the organization, each level of leader should be concerned with the success and growth of those below him or her on the organizational ladder. As each person ascends another rung, they should look to the rung below them to pull upward. Through this relationship of trust and mentorship, the organization continues to develop and advance its leaders. All organizations deserve to be led by an individual or team with a genuine desire to do good things for their followers but often, that is not the case. Many people have stories of the corrupting influence of a leader that changed the trajectory of their careers.

Participant Harold described a situation that he experienced when working as a mid-level manager in a large corporation dealing with an upper-level leader who appeared to be corrupted by power and, perhaps, his sense of self-preservation. Rather than encouraging, supporting, or mentoring his subordinate, this man, we will call "Tony" manipulated his subordinate and lied to him. The false information "Tony" spread influenced Harold's career decision. He was manipulated into a decision he would not have made. The importance of the trusted relationship with a leader, and the organizational harm wrought by an untrustworthy leader, is illustrated by this experience.

> The most devasting advice I received turned out to be a total lie. This was a lie told to me by my boss. He told me in the strictest confidence that the entire department was moving to New Jersey. He said he was letting me know ahead of time, but it was a lie. I took a (severance) package when it was offered. We had three major projects at that time, and I was responsible for two of them. These were really major projects. I felt that he wanted to get rid of anyone that would make it easier for them to fire him because the work would keep going on without him, (H.G. 2022).

In his real-life experience, Harold demonstrates how corrupt leaders will act in their own best interest even if it is detrimental to the organization and horribly consequential for an individual. This is the kind of person who should not have authority over others nor be in a position to make significant decisions for an organization. The lack of character, and the drive to self-preservation caused a re-direction that would never have occurred. Suggesting that a relocation was about to occur would cause most individuals to consider options, particularly if that person has a family. Uprooting an entire family and moving to a place the individual or family does not want to live is a disruption many would choose to avoid. When "Tony" misled Harold with false information, it caused Harold to believe he was going to have to move or be let go from the organization. He chose to leave on his own rather than having to face a relocation. Two major projects suffered the loss of a committed manager due to a deceitful senior leader.

Abuse of Power

Many Americans have a low opinion of politicians. Some Americans basically checked-out of the political process and stopped voting. People became discouraged with what they saw as elitism on both sides of the aisle. The D.C. entrenched seemed very disconnected to the rest of us across the country, particularly the working class. What we perceived as privilege of the elite turned out to be more a whole system of preferential treatment. At the start of the second term of President Donald Trump, he appointed Elon Musk to lead a team to uncover cases of waste, fraud, and abuse in the government. They very quickly found numerous cases of enormous waste of taxpayer dollars. Cases of corruption and abuse of power have come to light in large part due to the efforts of the Department of Government Efficiency (DOGE).

Regardless of political party, or level of government, examples of abuse of power and corruption can often be found. Each election, however, many of the same candidates get re-elected. There is frustration with politicians, yet change is difficult. Unseating a long-term incumbent can seem impossible. Wang and Sun (2015) conducted three studies showing different concepts in power and different implications for corruption, corrupting behavior and the perception of corruption. Their studies indicated a correlation between those who engage in corruption and the level of tolerance in general towards corruption (Wang & Sun, 2015). It appears, based on the research they have conducted, that people who are willing to engage in corruption are also willing to ignore others and live surrounded by corruption without concern. In other words, it is part of the culture and accepted as such. Perhaps Americans have become immune to the corruption and have adopted an attitude of acceptance. Many people do not engage in the political process. Could it be due to discouragement or disillusionment?

This cultural acceptance might explain the culture of waste, fraud, and abuse that is endemic in our government. As DOGE works hard to expose these things, there are elected officials fighting against their efforts. One would think that the reduction of waste, fraud, and abuse in the system would garner near universal support. Most Americans are cheering for the team intent on providing better governance over the budget. Most taxpayers are thrilled that someone is finally caring about the amount of hard-earned income that is wasted when it is sent to the government coffers. Why some people are against stopping the waste is indeed curious.

In American politics, many people become immersed in the "beltway culture" and rooted in their power. Corruption, based on their findings, would be closely tied to the environment and the level of tolerance for unethical behavior, as opposed to being directly tied to power. However, the connection could be made if the corrupt environment starts with the leadership. If unethical behavior is modeled and tolerated by leadership, corruption will flourish.

Political Power

Giovannoni and Seidmann (2013) conducted research on corruption looking specifically at democracies and the democratic process. They began with Acton's dictum which is basically the simple concept that power corrupts, and absolute power corrupts absolutely. Starting with this, they looked at various political elections to determine if Acton's dictum is true, and then, if it is true, is the opposite also true? In other words, they were considering the possibility that those without power are likely to be more honorable than those with power. Their research looked at voting and citizen response to corruption and they created a model to measure the effect of corruption and to quantify the amount of impact on behavior. They looked at the longevity of people remaining in political office, and the connection between incumbency and corruption. Their theory was that the longer the elected official stays in power, the more corrupt they become. They further built models testing the response of citizens. Within their construct, they concluded that coalitions form in response to a corrupt government and the likelihood of an incumbent being turned out of office is correlated to the amount of corruption perceived by the constituents.

Giovannoni and Seidmann (2013) concluded, "the corrupting effects of power affects power by allowing the state to change. If corruption is salient enough, then citizens turn out government" (Giovannoni and Seidmann, 2013, p. 15). In other words, if people are frustrated with politicians and aware of the abuse of power, they are more likely to work to get them removed from office. Once people become aware of the corruption, we should see more people voting and supporting outsiders to replace incumbents. The more informed the electorate becomes, the more accountable the elected officials will be.

One of the significant implications of research on corruption and power is the importance of the democratic system. Power remains with the people through the exercise of voting. Civil society with structured governance, a lawful citizenry, and the election process provides the people with a method of removing corrupt government actors. The notion of government working for the people rather than the people working for the government, when working as intended, should provide democratic countries with tools to prevent the abuse of power. The rights and freedoms provided by the American Constitution are intended to protect the country against the rise of authoritarianism. The socialist system, favored by some in this country, would allow for the imposition of tyranny. Socialism naturally invites those who are driven to control and those who crave power. Some people specifically desire power for the purpose of holding that power over the powerless (Gohler, 2009).

There is a difference between "power to" and "power over" that helps us understand the intent (Gohler, 2009). The concept of "power to" relates to independence and autonomy. This is the desire for an individual to be self-managed and free of constraint. The "power to" notion is generally considered positive. Most Americans believe in self-sufficiency and the strength of an independent actor and thinker. This is a distinctly different motivation than the "power over" concept, according to Gohler (2009). Those that desire to have power over others are driven to have a relationship with people where they are subject to the will of the power holder. This is generally considered a negative aspect of power (Gohler, 2009). "On the one hand, power to creates autonomy, while, on the other, power over limits the field of action" (Gohler, 2009, p. 29).

"Power over" allows one to impose his or her opinions, ideas, preferences, or plans without equal input from any other participants. Power can close off options otherwise available to those subjected to the powerful. Power can halt progress or stop speech. Power in the hands of those who have a voracious appetite for power over others can be incredibly dangerous to an organization or entity.

Power at Work

In business, does the same phenomena occur as what the research indicated about government? Is a CEO with longer tenure more prone to corruption than one who has been in the position just a few years? Is an organization with regular turnover in leadership better positioned than those companies retaining the same leaders in the same positions for decades? Does the power become more enticing over time? For some, there is never enough power, and they seem to be always looking for more. Any additional power just serves to increase the appetite for more power in an endless cycle.

Perhaps one indicator is the confidence and security a CEO has in his or her position. If they do not fear any consequences, they may feel more emboldened to take risks and engage in activities that are questionable, or corrupt. In theory at least, voters have the ability to remove an undesirable political leader from office. Employees typically do not have any "vote" on retention of their CEO or other leaders. If long-term leadership is problematic and likely to result in more corruption at the top, the entire organization suffers. Corruption and unethical behavior can then seep through the organizational layers down through the hierarchy until the entire organization becomes rotten.

Corruption can be more about greed and monetary benefits than power itself (Navot 2016). Navot (2016) tries to define political corruption in its various forms. Injustice can be the result of systemic, cultural corruption, or due to one powerful individual actor. Navot's (2016) work also points out the importance of morality in leadership. Navot (2016) questions how moral attitudes would influence corrupt behaviors. Moral attitudes should be considered critically important for leaders in both politics and business. In addition to the drive for power to have power over others, the drive for personal gain or financial enrichment can provide another incentive for corrupt behavior. Navot (2016) states that he is hoping to encourage more researchers and scholars to look at questions of ethics and morality, "independent of agents' wills and local norms, public opinion and how societies regulate political behavior" (Navot, 2016 p. 545).

If the problem of corruption cannot be addressed by logic and reason alone but must take morality into consideration, then morality must be addressed by hiring manager and human resources staff during the interview process and throughout subsequent development and advancement decisions for each employee. Sadly, many organizations do not take such things into consideration. When hiring a CEO, those making the hiring decision may want to consider character and ethics even more so than experience or skills. Hiring someone with a solid moral compass may be the most successful way to protect the organization from corruption. If we consider that reliance on experience and education will not guarantee the quality of the leader, a different approach to selecting leaders may be appropriate. Rather than focusing on organizational accomplishments from previous roles, perhaps a closer look at the personal accomplishments or attitudes. Prioritizing the ethics of a leader may result in a higher quality of leadership across the political and corporate landscape. The entire leadership landscape could evolve with improved interest in values and ethics.

A universal understanding or a moral culture is impossible if it relies on individual opinion, sentiment, or feelings. Moral relativism simply does not work. Our popular culture likes to perpetuate the idea that "your truth" and "my truth" can be different but they are both valid. This is a lie that has been thrust into the mainstream. There is one truth.

Navot (2016) notes the difference between what would be considered corruption or corrupting behaviors versus a law designed to eliminate corruption. Can you be engaging in an ethical act by violating the law? He questions if someone is in violation of a law, is it the same as corruption itself? Another interesting area of inquiry is the difference between morality and legality in terms of corruption. "Sometimes wrongness or rightness is a function of whether the government or organization has the capacity to ensure that some citizens or employees are not dominated by others, or even whether the entity in itself is becoming an oppressive element" (Navot, 2016).

In politics it can depend on who is in office and what laws they prioritize and which laws the powerful choose to ignore. Recent events exemplify this reality. While many cities were looted, burned, and attacked during the George Floyd protests and rioting most perpetrators were not punished. While the actions of those individuals were minimized, the same government power sought to imprison pastors and others praying publicly for unborn babies. These are the choices of government separate from ethics. In 2025, the government is choosing to enforce immigration law. Those in violation of the law are facing consequences that they would not have faced under the previous administration or even under the opposition political party. There are two completely opposite applications of the law, which would seem impossible given that the law has not changed. What has changed is who holds the power.

If an organization is oppressive, then we need to consider how they gained the power to be oppressive. In a democratic system it should be highly unusual for people to choose to vote for candidates who have expressed a preference for a system that would restrict freedom and self-determination, such as socialism. Any form of government that includes central planning means a loss of freedom for most and an amassing of power by the few. Anyone advancing socialist or communist philosophies likely intends on imposing oppressive authority. There are certainly many individuals who would gravitate naturally to the role of dictator. As unlikely as it seems, elected officials who favor a socialist or centralized form of government are gaining popularity in the United States.

Congressman Bernie Sanders (D-VT), who finds communism an appealing system, continues to be popular. Congresswoman Alexandria Ocasio-Cortez (D-NY) has risen to enormous popularity espousing a socialist ideology. It is difficult to comprehend why free people with rights and privileges would be so easily convinced that living under an authoritarian power could be a better way of life. One theory is they simply don't know any better.

Without a solid knowledge of history, many millennials and generation Z have no personal knowledge of the terror of communism. Younger generations missed the years of the USSR and the Cold War. It would appear that history classes have not covered the horrors of communist takeovers of several countries in recent history. There seems to be a deficit of history lessons in the current public-school curriculum. If they knew and understood how socialist philosophies have played out in reality, they would certainly not be advocating for the way of life that so many in Cuba, China, and N. Korea risked their lives to escape.

Ego and Arrogance

Perhaps corrupt leaders are disillusioned or living in their own world. In their superior position and power, they are blind to their own behavior. Johnston (2013) points out that corrupt leaders also have the ability to disregard their own failings. "Elite miscreates can usually deny that they have acted in corrupt ways" (Johnston, 2013, p. 1247). If the leader cannot recognize their own failings, most people in the leader's sphere of influence can easily identify an abuse of power. Acting on it, however, takes courage. Many employees are likely to remain hopeful for change in their boss rather than seeking to make a change themselves. Positive power can inspire and energize. Tyrannical power can hinder and hurt. An important step towards recognizing and understanding the situation you find yourself in is understanding power.

Ego plays a significant role in leadership. We all want to be viewed positively by our peers and our teams. We want to go home at the end of the day and believe we have had accomplishments and successes. Participant Mark said there's often a need to win or a feeling that winning is important. He cautions that focusing too much on winning can be detrimental. Leaders are also driven by a fear of failure. Leaders need to take risks without being frozen by the prospect of failure. Failure can be a great teacher.

> You feel like you have to win all the time and failure is something you just don't ever want to see. So, we fear failure, but I think as I did fail on some things you really can learn from those failures. You need to be able to handle failure. I think that's the most critical part because if you fail and it just destroys you emotionally and takes just takes the wind out of your sails that's a problem. If you're surrounded by people that allow you to fail and use that to build you can get in front of the failures and learn from them (M. H., 2022).

Some leaders avoid making difficult decisions or taking bold action because they fear what will happen if they fail. They do not want to look bad, and the ego drives the behavior. Rather than experiencing and benefitting from taking risks, they avoid it for their own protection. "My first failure, I learned a lot. I learned a tremendous amount. Then, the turning point for me was realizing that it's ok, these things happen. This is what happens in business, and we learn from the mistakes. People are always afraid to make mistakes or look bad" (M. H., 2022).

> We need to be willing to listen even if what someone is telling us even if it is a blow to the ego. Humility is very valuable for a leader to have. Particularly it is often difficult for subordinates to tell a leader something he or she does not want to hear. Refusing to listen and recognize an opportunity for a change or correction is to our detriment.

That person may not be right, but they should be heard. Check your ego at the door. Be sure you are not unwilling to listen because you are not willing to consider that you may be wrong or may have made an error, or that someone simply has a better idea than you do. Many of us have fallen into the trap of thinking we know best. We should listen to others with an open mind.

Bases of Power

French and Raven (1959) developed their theories on the bases of power. Bertram Raven continued with additional research on the topic of power bases and the update to the original work and adds a sixth power base, informational power, to the original five bases of power. This describes how leaders influence followers to obtain compliance with a directive or direction. According to Raven (2008), the six bases of power include Informational, Reward, Coercive, Legitimate, Expert, and Referent. Leaders with any of the six bases of power would have the ability to engage in corruption or corrupt behaviors, however, we can consider each of the powers in terms of the impact on employees.

The two socially dependent bases of power are reward power and coercive power. The target is dependent upon the person with the power and the punishment or reward can be directly connected to the act of compliance or non-compliance. Legitimate power results in compliance when the target believes that the person in power has the right to ask what he or she is asking for. Expert power involves a person with a level of knowledge that is respected by the target. This leader instills confidence due to the extent of their expertise. The target will follow because he or she is confident in the knowledge of the leader. Referent power results when the target identifies with the leader and aspires to be like the leader. This may be a role model to those he or she leads (Pierro & Raven, 2008).

Raven (2008) attempted to begin addressing the question of how a power base is chosen. He states that simple compliance is not always the goal and does not always determine which power base is chosen. A leader may choose a different power base for different results. He refers to other researchers exploring the need for affiliation, need for power and need for achievement. Choosing a particular power base, therefore, is about the leader and his or her needs and drives. It may even simply be a decision influenced by the level of self-esteem. Understanding the follower does not seem important if the leader is more interested in serving himself or herself, which each of these things do. Affiliation, achievement, and power are all about the individual leader, not about the citizenry or constituency they serve.

Raven explains how the different power bases are likely to be selected given the influences mentioned above. Raven states, "A leader or supervisor with a high need for power will be more likely to select Impersonal Coercive Power and Legitimate Position Power. Those with strong affiliation needs, and concern that their subordinate will like them, will more likely prefer Referent Power and Reward Power, especially Personal Reward Power. A need for achievement might result in more use of Informational and Expert Power" (Raven, 2008, p.5).

While we don't always understand the impact, we can often identify controlling, authoritarian leaders. Where we see strong central control, we also see the type of leader who likely exhibits a tendency towards a coercive power base. If the coercive or tyrannical nature of the individual can be determined more clearly, perhaps people would choose to work for different leaders.

According to Chandler & Kirsch (2018), there is no way to escape oppression. It is always in existence in a structured society. They further explain that those in leadership positions will remain in leadership positions by, "enforcing and encoding certain norms, habits, and assumptions" (Chandler & Kirsch, 2018, p. 177). Leaders who can use power effectively can be far more successful than those who do not know how to wield power. Weak leaders who do not know how to implement positive power techniques will cause confusion, instability, and distrust in an organization. Those who regularly, arbitrarily, engage in excessive authoritarianism risk alienating or demoralizing employees. Both ends of the spectrum are undesirable.

If politicians are largely leading through coercive power, legislation they create tends to rely on coercive power as well. Hartley and Bennington (2011) state, "political leadership carries the coercive power of the state, and their use of such power has to demonstrate that it is 'fair' thus making the connection between the power base, coercive power, and 'fairness' or what we might extend to justice (p. 207). We can also see this in other organizations. You may recognize those leading through coercive power as those relying on the organization for punishment. That leader will remind the follower that he or she is more powerful and has the ability to force compliance or inflict consequences for non-compliance. A threat can be subtle or direct. It can be the unspoken awareness that one's job depends on the leader willing to continue to support and retain the employee. A powerful leader using coercion can make sure that a non-compliant employee does not gain a promotion or opportunities for development. If you are in a situation where your manager is threatening your job, you should already be looking for another one.

Hartley and Bennington (2011) addressed the evolution of political leadership from earlier times when political leaders were known for "wisdom and virtue" (p. 205). In these earlier years, politicians were expected to be above reproach. They use the example of the "divine rights" of kings in previous ruling governments. This was a time when leaders were not elected, but elevated (Hartley & Bennington, 2011). Also, in the Hartley and Bennington article, there is reference to the authority of the political leader, so this may connect to the legitimate power base.

Johnston (2013) states that governments hold "unique powers of coercion" so the opportunity for corruption is vast (p. 240). Government leaders can punish citizens and have unlimited resources to pursue any noncompliant person. Consider the case of the IRS agents who targeted conservative groups, investigating them to the point of essentially crushing their ability to function (Schatz 2015). Review the decision by the state of Tennessee that arbitrarily required African American hair braiders to have a cosmetology license. Women who had engaged in this business for many years suddenly, with the swipe of a government pen, were out of business until completing a year of cosmetology school (Flatten, 2017).

Reflect on the vast number of violations found within the Veteran's Administration (Slack & Estes, 2018). Veterans were neglected and when corruption was reported, the administrators retaliated (Slack & Estes, 2018). Administrators were able to leverage power with the full weight of the United States Government behind them. Veterans had trusted the government, given the VA power over their health and well-being, and they were effectively abandoned by a bureaucracy with coercive power and extensive authority over patients dependent upon the VA. Veterans were abandoned by the system designed to provide them care, (Westwood, 2016). Johnston (2013) comments that with so many organizations and opportunities, we should not be questioning why we have so much corruption, but why we don't have more.

Corrupt leaders at the top of a private organization can influence public policy and corrupt leaders, even in smaller organizations, can still do damage. According to Donald J. Boudreaux, a senior fellow with American Institute for Economic Research, corruption may not happen as frequently in business as it does in politics due to the level of oversight. Boudreaux says incompetence and corruption are almost commonplace among political leaders, but not so among business leaders. Bourdreaux (2022) says politicians, "have long peddled nonsense to their constituents". Business executives do not have the ability to cover up their evidence of failure as politicians do (Bourdreaux, 2022). Additionally, Bourdreaux (2022) reasons that there are expectations of politicians that they "work miracles" thus pressuring them to find solutions that may not even make sense. Private employers do not have the same magic wand and access to the pot of gold, i.e., taxpayer dollars. Business leaders often have a range of people to respond to. They may have shareholders, customers, suppliers and vendors, community members and a board of directors. While a CEO may have a great deal of authority and autonomy, if things go horribly wrong, and if it becomes known, they could face serious consequences. If problems can remain hidden a CEO or senior leader may avoid consequences for a substantial amount of time, but probably not forever.

Preparing for Power

Power will always exist in organizations. Power and influence are necessary to lead. It's how a leader applies power that matters. Positive power can energize and excite a team to go above and beyond. Negative power can result in conflict within the team, backstabbing and scapegoating, and a generally unhealthy culture. As a leader it's important to learn how to use power positively avoiding coercive tendencies. Particularly for new leaders, the coercive approach tends to be a crutch. Until a leader becomes more skilled and confident, he or she may rely on the weight of the organization's capabilities for penalties rather than the appeal of his or her own leadership style.

When trying to work collaboratively with your senior leader, it's important to understand how your manager is exerting control. If you can determine which power base your boss uses, you can better understand his or her leadership style and how to respond to it. Reward power is very common and an easy system for most employees to work within. Better performance results in better rewards. That is a reasonable working culture for most people. Legitimate power is also easily understood. Those at the top of the organizational structure will have more influence than those at the bottom. That system also tends to be comfortable for many employees as it is open and straightforward. It also can motivate those who would like more authority to achieve what is necessary to advance to higher positions in the organizational structure. Once a person achieves a higher position in the organizational structure, more power is earned.

If the leader is driven by a need for power or achievement, he or she will almost certainly use the coercive power base engaging in fear tactics and pressure to maintain compliance. As mentioned previously, some people crave power and can be driven to unusual, or even unethical, behavior to maintain power. For the power hungry, other individuals can represent a threat to their power. They will often not allow dissent, or even discussion, fearing their own exposure. They will oppress an entire organization into servitude if necessary. As Gordon (2011) explains, people who crave power do not like to be challenged. Ineffective leaders cannot risk being surrounded by those with the freedom and knowledge to question authority. To ensure their supremacy, the leader may create such an intimidating environment that employees fear speaking up about anything.

There are many examples of leaders who have become more powerful than practical and more greedy than ethical. Those who refuse to fall in line when faced with these leaders will find themselves in a precarious position in the organization. The only ones who can succeed in a culture led by a coercive, power-hungry boss are those willing to just do what they are told. Independent thinkers will not be embraced in this culture. There are some people who will find this arrangement very comfortable. It can be very easy to go along and get along. If you just agree with whatever is presented and tell the boss what he or she wants to hear, all will be well with your world. Divert from that, however, and you will find yourself in an untenable position. One must remain compliant and agreeable in this arrangement.

Beyond coercive power, there are other power bases that also can be used detrimentally. If a leader has a strong need for affiliation and acceptance, they may use reward power inappropriately to gain loyalty from subordinates. They want to be liked, and they can use the company expense account to buy friends. This leader is focused on his own her own popularity. They worry if someone does not seem to like them and they gravitate to those who make them feel good about themselves. To help the process along, this type of leader may offer rewards beyond what other employees can earn. Favoritism can become an issue for those relying on reward power to manage a staff or team. If one employee or one team seems to be getting perks, raises, or some other unusual accommodation, others in the organization are likely to notice, and be annoyed. What about the other team members who may not be involved in the current project or program? What about the reliable employee who is not politically or socially skilled, or who just chooses not to engage in false compliments and fawning over the boss?

Another problem occurs if the "favored" employees become accustomed to their privileges. Those privileges can quickly become entitlements. If some employees have been conditioned to expect rewards and the entire power and influence base of the leader relies on rewarding employees, what happens when a reward is not given? Do employees continue to do the job they are paid to do, or do they begin to become apathetic in the absence of the carrot dangling in front of them?

One indication of the type of power you are dealing with is to determine what this manager or leader has done for employees in the past. Ask those who have the longest tenure about their experience. Look around within the facility. Do employees have certificates of recognition at their desk or displayed around their workstations? Do people look uncomfortable when the boss walks through or do they take the time to stop what they are doing and greet him or her? How often are raises given? Do people seem to respect authority or disregard it? Does the leader seem self-absorbed? Is he or she shamelessly promoting himself or herself? Do leaders regularly publicly praise individuals who have done an exceptional job? Do subordinates easily engage in discussions with leaders, even if they offer a different opinion?

If you are already in a position of authority, we would suggest that you use power and influence wisely. Developing the ability to recognize power bases will help you become more intentional when choosing how to use power and influence. You can be aware of your own instincts and correct them if they are not healthy or beneficial. Recognize what you are trying to accomplish and deliberately determine how much pressure needs to be applied. How do you know how much pressure and influence will be effective in motivating the employee? A leader will struggle answering these questions if he or she does not know the individuals reporting to him or her. If you don't know your employees, you don't really know how much influence is necessary.

Some employees are intrinsically motivated and need very little influence to perform at their best level. Encouragement, support, and an expression of appreciation will go a long distance with this type of employee. Other employees may need more pressure and application of influence tactics (Tjosvold & Wisse, 2009). They may be more responsive to reward power (French & Raven, 1959). The employee who is more motivated by the hope of a reward needs external influence to perform. They may be looking for a salary increase, promotion or a bonus. They may desire public recognition.

For most employees it is generally advised to offer appreciation for a job well done. In the fast-paced world most of us live in, it is easy to forget to acknowledge employee contributions. It is incumbent upon all leaders to remember to frequently provide recognition when it is warranted. When employees stay late, put in extra effort, display teamwork, it is essential to recognize those who go above and beyond. It does not have to be a physical reward, but just an appreciation of thanks. If providing rewards, they must be defined and clearly stated so any employee can see why this reward was given to this person. It is important for the employee being rewarded, and it is an example for other employees to follow. An outstanding employee can then be a role model for the entire team.

Our participants made this point clearly. Each of them described the importance of appreciating the teams that report to you. Harold said it is essential to recognize the staff and appreciate them as they will be the ones that ensure your success or failure as a leader (H.G., 2022). Knowing what it is that drives an employee's behavior is critical and incredibly valuable to a leader. If you know the employee responds to rewards, preparing regular incentives is beneficial. "Effective leaders use performance-contingent reward power to increase job satisfaction and performance of subordinates" (Rahim, 2009, p. 236).

Understand what motivates your employees. Are they more likely to follow you if there is a reward for them? Are they more likely to become engaged if they can expect to be promoted for their efforts? Some people require a more strategic approach to influence motivation. There are employees who like to push the envelope. Proper use of power tactics can make a major difference in the success of a challenging employee (Tjosvold & Wisse, 2009). The goal is to seek compliance, so the employee succeeds in a task or in his or her role, and the organization benefits from his or her performance. "Compliance can be said to occur when the influencing agent's power exceeds the target's resistance" (Koslowsky & Schwarzwals, 2009, p. 244).

Most people prefer not to use tactics considered harsh; however, data suggests that often a more assertive approach has more impact., so it may be necessary to use tactics that may seem overwhelming to some. "Although harsh tactics are indeed less socially desirable, their judicial usage in certain cases may be beneficial without necessarily causing negative repercussions in the relationship" (Koslowsky & Schwarzwals, 2009, p. 250). An example of a harsh tactic would be the threat of punishment. For example, if an employee is not performing at the level required for his or her current job, a demotion might be suggested. Perhaps an employee might lose previously extended privileges such as attendance at a conference or event. When softer tactics are likely to be successful, they should be utilized first before ratcheting up to the harsher approach. This is why many organizations rely on progressive discipline. We want to attempt a lighter approach until it becomes necessary to do more. A leader relying too heavily on a harsh tactic or reacting too hastily to apply a harsh tactic may be one with low self-esteem or someone who is concerned about his or her own security in the organization (Koslowsky & Schwarzwals, 2009).

Motivating employees requires knowing your employees. Knowing how much power and what type of power will motivate them can lead to a more effective relationship between leader and follower. Use of power and influence is complicated, and the specter of corruption waits in the wings for those leaders who enjoy wielding power, not for organizational achievements, but for the enjoyment of the power itself. As leaders, we can do better by educating ourselves and practicing self-awareness. We can choose how to wield authority by recognizing the responsibilities, not just the rights and privileges, of power.

CHAPTER FOUR
POWER AND DECISIONS

Those who make decisions must have the power to do so. They must be authorized and have formal authority of leadership but, implementation of power is not a skill readily found, or easily trained. Many people in leadership roles are not prepared to use power wisely. Power can be the force that protects and improves the lives of those it governs, or it can create a miserable existence. According to Foucault (1982), people within an organization tend to blame the person directly over them when things go awry, never recognizing the higher authority. Within an organization we may not even know who is making us miserable. Confusion within the multiple layers of the hierarchy benefits those who would choose to use the organizational structure to hide their influence and assert control subversively. Who is exerting the power and how is it impacting each person and the organization?

Individual managers tend to be more inclined to hire and promote those with operational skills, rather than leadership abilities. Middle managers, in particular, are often extremely busy juggling pieces of the organizational chart both above and below. It is a very difficult role and navigating that role successfully includes fancy footwork. When there is an open position, managers are even more pressured to look at employees as operational functionaries, rather than human capital with potential. When hiring, managers are highly likely to favor the candidate that can fill the existing opening and hit the ground running. The long-term vision is often sacrificed to the short-term practical reality. A person with more long-term potential may not get hired regardless of the benefit to the organization.

Another problem that reduces the leadership capacity of an organization is the suppression of those with the very traits and skills needed to grow into leadership roles. Candidates with leadership skills may intimidate a manager and thus not get hired. Employees with leadership traits may also find themselves in the crosshairs of their manager.

Employees may be deliberately excluded from advancement if the only person who has the authority to determine career pathing for their subordinates is the direct manager. Managers may have a vested interest in keeping a quality employee in their current role because he or she makes the manager look better. It is certainly preferable for a manager to keep a good employee in a role than to have to find someone new and train them. Managers may also disregard employees that make them feel uncomfortable. Strong personalities and those with traits of a leader can intimidate those they report to. A manager may fear a person who may take some of the spotlight. Through subtle messaging, or outright hostility, potential or even existing leaders may be chased out of an organization by anyone more concerned with protecting their own dominance rather than in advancing and ensuring the longevity of the organization. This is another reason that leadership development must be strategic and selective

Those with power can impact organizations and individuals. Most people have expectations of those with power. They are viewed as the stewards of our careers, our income, and the direction of our organizational life. The success of failure can be due to the powerful players in our lives and their decision-making. We trust those in power to use the authority given to do the best job they can for the organization they are responsible for. "Power is received in the promise of fulfilling expectations – people in authority, we insist, must provide direction, protection, and order" (Heifetz, 1994, p.125). Heifetz (1994) says this is reasonable and logical. We should expect leaders to have power and to use it wisely. "Procedures, lines of authority, role placements, and norms of operation have been established. People have a sufficiently clear idea about what needs to be done and how to go about doing it" (Heifetz, 1994, p. 125).

Authority can become a "straight jacket" however when change and adaptation is needed. When our leaders do not act quickly enough, they often get blamed. It is typical to blame authority figures when things do not seem to go the way we expect (Heifetz, 1994).

In a world that moves ever quicker thanks to the speed of technology and with companies growing, changing, and fighting to stay relevant and competitive, how can employees be clear about their level of authority and their ability to make decisions within their structure? If individuals in an organization cannot determine who is asserting authority over them, the potential for hidden power and corruption exists, along with the opportunity to create a general sense of confusion. While structure is critical, are leaders effectively able to manage structure while providing the level of freedom and flexibility necessary for modern organizations to be successful? In complex organizations, power can be the arbitrator between freedom and restriction.

When faced with growth and change, the organization can become chaotic and confusing. The lack of clarity can result in an abuse of power by those seeking to acquire power when a chaotic environment presents an opportunity. A player without real authority may find space to assert his or her agenda during times of disorder. Anarchy presents opportunities for those seeking such chances.

Modern Organizations and Complexity

Legitimate power may no longer be sustainable in an age where "hierarchical lines of authority will be questioned" (Axelrod & Cohen, 2000, p. 29). Perhaps, in modern and future organizations, we need to reconsider the control parameters and adjust to the complex environment (Byrne & Callaghan, 2014). An approach accepting complexity and recognizing complex systems might require a different balance between control and freedom, structure, and agency (Byrne & Callaghan, 2014). All types of organizations struggle with this problem. In addition to the potential for losing creative freedom and innovation, followers may become frustrated with leadership if the power direction appears convoluted. This confusion provides an opportunity for political positioning and an outsized influence on decisions.

The use, or abuse, of power is one of the most concerning aspects of decision-making. Once one has the authority to unilaterally make a decision, what if they neglect to consider the consequences of their decision, particularly consequences beyond those that influence the decision-maker? How do we, as leaders, refrain from abuse of power? Those who lead from a position of strength may, even inadvertently, be blind to the impact on others. Taking time to think through outcomes and potential outcomes may slow the decision-making but may prevent unintended consequences. This is the balancing act of power. Determining when speed and efficiency outweigh the time-consuming, measured approach.

Leaders are expected to make decisions and manage power within their own organizations, but it may be far more complicated than we realize in our increasingly fast-paced, ever more complex world (Uhl-Bien & Marion, 2011). Does anyone know what the optimal power balance is between leader and follower? The problem becomes more concerning when we consider that many people are given authority without those qualities we might hope to see in a leader, using their power foolishly or in service to their own, potentially questionable, agenda. Even the most successful leaders in organizations can exhibit irrational or unethical behaviors (Kets de Vries & Balazs 2011).

Another skill to improve for those interested in making better decisions and being better leaders is the art of listening. Listening, not just to hear the answer to the question to listening with deeper understanding. Some people call it reading between the lines. This type of listening requires discernment. We, as leaders, cannot just listen and accept words at face value. We should be watching body language, facial expressions, and accept information in the context of the culture, the history, and the individual background of the person providing the information. Some people give an answer without the knowledge necessary to really respond. Some will have hidden agendas. Some will outright lie. Some will not be forthcoming for one reason or another. It is important to listen not just to hear, but to understand. "I try to help people understand. Seek first to understand. I try to lead them down the path. With employees I help them decide which way to go. As a leader that's really the best you can do is to do your best and give the best advice" (M. H., 2022).

Many people in leadership lack the skills to really be effective in their role. Consider the way people are often promoted. Typically, promotion into leadership comes from success in doing the work. Those who are successful doing a particular job do not necessarily make good leaders. Promotion to management is often a reward for hard work, which seems reasonable, however, this is a mistake. Leadership requires different skills and often different traits than those who are successful in other areas. When an individual who is not blessed with the traits of a leader and not provided with the skills of a leader becomes a leader, it is no surprise that the outcome generally is not good. Those who have experienced success in their job are not always the same people who can effectively harness and manage power and authority. This may be most obvious when they are asked to make decisions.

Honest Debate or Dishonest Discussion

Power can be understood in terms of agency and collective agency. If one has the ability to disagree with those in power, then they have the freedom to share their opinions freely. Whether others in the organization have the freedom to discuss, debate, object, or provide any kind of feedback, then the organization has distributed power and provided for agency. This will make a significant difference in decision-making. If an organization seeks input, they can rely on the honesty of the team if they have created an environment that encourages honest feedback. If the leaders have not effectively created an environment where the employees feel free to express an opinion, then they will not benefit from their knowledge. Additionally, they may be misled if they assume support simply based on silence. Employees who know that their manager is getting ready to make a mistake will not often risk his or her own job to offer an opinion if the culture has punished those who engage without acceptance and submission.

If power is wielded in a corrosive or oppressive manner, and employees have accepted that their honest feedback is not important, they will keep their comments to themselves. Protecting themselves and their jobs become the priority. Within these organizations, employees will often feel demoralized and devalued and therefore, unlikely to confidently express a position during a decision-making process. People will just conform, agree, and follow mindlessly in the numb world of irrelevance. Those not conforming to the organizationally accepted behavior may be rejected, ostracized, or punished with lack of resources or support. (Axelrod & Cohen, 2000). If organizational leaders would like a decision or discussion to include a wide range of thoughts and ideas, they need to create a culture that encourages employee contributions. The parameters of a decision-making process can be clear. When input is sought, it should be honest.

There should be no consequences for disagreeing with a leader, as long as it is done respectfully. Senior leaders need to set the tone by controlling their own power and influence recognizing how intimidating that can be to others in the room. If a leader wants to encourage independent thought and creative approaches brought by a multitude of different perspectives, it will take preparation and a strategic approach to decision-making (Griffin-Ray, 2022). If this does not happen, you risk crushing an idea that just might be the one that launches the organization or department into the next level of success.

Power is assigned through formal structure and job titles, but informal power can be exerted through social networks and relationships. Some of these networks and social systems create a shadow leadership blurring the distinction between legitimate and illegitimate power (Dean, 2009). Those adapting to the structure may not even be aware whether they are responding to formal leadership or informal leadership. The complex system where power can be hidden is what is often misunderstood.

Power is either represented clearly or by an anonymous, unknown person or structure (Torfing, 2009). Within the hierarchy, power is adapting, adjusting, and emerging as new individuals enter the system and other people leave. Organizations typically experience staffing adjustments on a regular basis. Depending on the size and the stability of the organization, new people can join the organization regularly as existing employees leave through retirement, resignation, or termination. When turnover occurs in an organization, often power struggles emerge between competing entities. A settlement will eventually occur, and a new entity emerges (Byrne & Callaghan, 2014).

Leaders skilled in decision-making will use their authority to guide others towards their way of thinking. The art form is constructing the environment most conducive to effective decision-making. How much power should a leader assert while attempting to involve others in an honest discussion? If leaders want contributions from employees, they must know that they can contribute without fear of reprisal. A healthy discussion should include ground rules and guidelines, so participants are not surprised. Debate can be healthy as long as everyone understands the rules. The person facilitating the meeting should introduce the meeting, describe the purpose and the intended outcome, and frame the decision so each participant knows what is expected of him or her. At the end of the discussion, if the intent is to conclude with a decision, it should be explained that the final decision is the final decision. It may not be the decision you prefer, but you must accept it when the final decision is made. Once the process is concluded, the person tasked with implementation should begin the work of engaging support and compliance. As a leader attempts to gain compliance, according to Martins (2017), transparency and clarity of purpose and intent would likely be more successful.

Weber (1994) noted that authoritarian power evolves, in part, due to confusion of the power structure. If established ahead of time, there should be no confusion about the plan for the decision, the process to make it, and the power levels and authority. In other words, if a decision is made based on a vote, then the majority will be the final arbiter of the decision. If the final decision is made by a smaller team, or one individual, that should be disclosed so there is no disappointment or resentment. If the final decision will be made by one person, than that should be disclosed during the decision process.

Leaders can develop better processes for decision-making when they are deliberate about it. Before a meeting is called, determine if this meeting should end with a decision. If so, who needs to be in that room? Who needs to be included in the decision? What data do we need to make this decision? What is the timeline to make this decision? If we discover that we would like more data, additional people, or external guidance, maybe we should defer the decision making to a later time. Is it even a decision that needs to be made? Is it really necessary that I make this decision? Is there a timeline that must be met, or is there flexibility when the decision needs to be made? Providing clear guidelines on the decision making process will improve outcomes for the organization and the individual stakeholders.

Rules, Restrictions and Regulation

Managers who exert too much power and influence risk demoralizing the employee and restricting their interest in participating in decision making or contributing to the organization in any way. Appropriate use of power and the process of decision making is developed over time. Delegating power and sharing a decision-making process is not always easy for leaders, particularly in a high risk or highly regulated environment.

The releasing of restrictive controls and unleashing of entrepreneurial ability has been a driver of economic success and this environment is often the aspiration of innovative organizations (Hayek, 2007). Modern organizations, exemplified particularly in technology companies, benefit significantly from the ability to capitalize on the ingenuity of their technologically gifted talent. Some of the concern leaders have in delegating authority and decision making is the consequences of violating a law or regulation. Regulatory controls are another layer of complexity added to a leader's process for leading and decision making.

Government gives us an example of the power used to drive behaviors and compliance. Any government authority has some need to demand compliance for the citizenry, but at the same time, a free society must remain free and unincumbered from oppressive tactics. As former British Prime Minister, Margaret Thatcher (2002) said, "But government in a free society must also be limited in size and scope: it must not intrude into those aspects of life which are by rights private; and, above all, it must uphold and abide by, not undermine, or override, the law. The call for 'strong measures' and 'strong men' is often an all too well-known preliminary to some kind of dictatorship" (p. 105).

Understanding the balance is the charge of those in authority in free societies. Power in a bureaucracy offers many places to hide and, ironically, it is difficult to escape the power of the state. Those in power can exert a great deal of influence and control over those who are not well positioned.

The concern of the burgeoning bureaucracy in the United States is the growth of power and the potential for abuse. The larger, and more complex, the more places for hidden power, corruption, and the development of a culture of non-decision (Griffin-Ray, 2022). Johnston (2013) states that governments hold "unique powers of coercion" so the opportunity for corruption is vast (p. 240). Governments have unlimited amounts of resources and can use as much capital as they determine is necessary to crush whatever opposition they encounter (Johnston, 2013). As Johnston (2013) points out, typically a government is a monopoly. This gives them unusual, and encompassing, power. According to Jessop (2011), however, the state does not have to resort to coercion if the state power is considered legitimate. The state, whether it asserts it or not, does have the ability to apply coercive methods so, is it really just legitimate power or is it hidden, coercive power? Jessop (2009) states, "Even when blessed with political legitimacy... many also rely heavily on force, fraud, and corruption and their subjects' inability to organize effective resistance" (p. 369).

Adam Smith (1976) described the prudent role of the state this way. "The wisdom of every state or commonwealth endeavors, as well as it can, to employ the force of the society to restrain those who are subject to its authority, from hurting or disturbing the happiness of one another" (p. 218). Governments as well as businesses and other types of organizations can consider their prudent role as well. Most organizations face the same need for control and compliance, while balancing freedom for creativity and innovation. Recognizing times where restraint is warranted is a quality of a well-managed organization. Creating a culture where "the good" infects all players and all projects and innovation, independent thinking, and effective collaboration can thrive.

The structure of the organization, like the state, is considered necessary, within balance, as a source to minimize chaos and to create order and equilibrium (Follett, 2016). Employees then should hold their leaders accountable. It might take an occasional reminder or nudge. Individuals choose to join a company and work in service towards the mission of that organization. It's a mutual agreement. Both sides have a responsibility to perform their respective roles. Power can be used positively to fuel the energy of the organization. Leaders may just need to be held accountable when the inevitable pressure of performance causes them to slip into their own organizational oblivion. An honest answer from a loyal employee is a great benefit to a leader. Those courageous enough to speak up when things are going wrong are the people who care enough to prioritize the health of the organization over their own wellbeing. Leaders should encourage risk taking for the benefit of the organization within reason. Each organization or department should know what level of risk is acceptable. There is no free ride in the organizational environment. Leaders must lead, but followers must also be good followers. In the next chapter we explain the importance of followership.

CHAPTER FIVE
LEADERS, FOLLOWERS AND STRUCTURE

Those born to lead seem to naturally accept the mantle. Those growing and working towards becoming leaders need to find role models and improve their own skills. First, anyone seeking a leadership role should gain a practical understanding of what exactly that entails. Many focus on the promotional aspects of management, forgetting the practical application of management. Once promoted, it is difficult to back down so many people stumble around and muddle through. Some basic understanding and guidance can help improve direction and confidence.

What really is the role of the leader? Mark explained the importance of having a vision and communicating a vision for followers.

> The leader's role is to develop the vision. Create a big picture for people to understand and follow. Managers need to see the vision. A manager has not really stepped into that leadership role unless he has the will or ability to create a vision. You know, some really couldn't capture the vision. It is partly, you know, afraid to kind of step into that role, because if we all know you know, being a leader as I always have full people, you know you have to risk being unpopular. In business, whether I agree with you or not, it's how you're going to do it. It's better if I agree

with what you're doing or how you're doing it. The problem is that some people think they are leaders, but they even struggle capturing the vision. That is going to spill. That's because I think those that have been able to really contrast that constant difference...I would say that that's probably the most critical is about the most critical concept that a leader. The leader has to be able to see the big picture. They can deal with the small picture, but really create the big the big vision, the big picture and then lead the group. Inspire the group (M.H., 2022).

Leaders in organizations are often placed in positions after earned accomplishments, or they are hired for known competencies. Once in the position, they are regularly engaged in improving their leadership skills. Leaders across the industry spectrum attend leadership seminars, read leadership books, and attend leadership workshops. In other words, leaders are constantly working on becoming better leaders and an entire industry has built up around this reality. How often, however, do you hear about employees trying to become better followers? Leaders cannot lead if others are unwilling to follow and without role clarity the group resides in a place of disorganization and chaos.

Most of us start our career following, not leading. The role of a follower is important, but it is rarely explained as a critical part of organizational functioning. While we are in a follower role, we do have responsibilities to accept direction, fulfill what is asked of us, respect our leader, and perform the tasks assigned to the best of our ability. Watching geese fly overhead we can observe an incredible art of organization where one is in the lead and others follow, in a very specific pattern. When milling about on the ground, a similar pattern emerges. One bird leads, gives a signal, or begins progressing to another location and the group quickly follows. The birds communicate in some way that allows all participants in the group to understand what is expected of them to fulfill their role. Successful organizations need leaders to lead but also must have followers willing to follow.

In my first professional role, I knew I was expected to be a follower. I needed to listen to those with more experience and take directions from my supervisor. I was prepared to do just that; however, followership was more complicated than I had expected. There were challenges and politics and, of course, my own ego was definitely in my way. I had an expectation of reporting to someone who would teach and train me and guide my career. I thought my immediate supervisor would take an interest in me, recognize my talent, and be excited to have me on the team. In reality, my supervisor was just glad to fill the role and get the job done. Like many people, she was just getting through the days one at a time and not particularly focused on the future. She certainly was not focused on my future.

This first professional experience was disappointing in many ways. The manager that I reported to was largely unavailable during a significant amount of the workday. Our team was small so she may have assumed we did not require much supervision. The company was large and spread across different buildings and our manager was often somewhere within the facility, but not near our department. There were many places people could be while still within the organizational parameters. These were the days before cell phones, so if a person was in a different building, or even a different part of a building, the only way to alert that person that they were needed was to use the intercom system and page them by name, which was incredibly intimidating, and probably a very bad idea when it was a subordinate looking for a supervisor. Even when the paging system was utilized, in some parts of the building, that was ineffective due to the noise. Generally, once someone was not seen, they were not accessible.

I understood that our manager had a role that took her to other departments, but I also noticed that she had a thriving social life at work. She had many friends and seemed to be well liked. She had been with the company many years and, if I remember correctly, I believe this was her first job and she had been there her entire career up to this point. I was told, and eventually noticed, that many of those in management acquired those roles, at least in part, due to popularity and the social network. The culture encouraged an environment where family members were hired, friends were promoted, and those outside of the inner circle were largely ignored. There were several lower-level managers who were known to have social ties with top leaders. It would do no good to question their decisions or direction as they all had connections. This environment made it difficult to be a loyal follower.

Someone might question what harm it would do for people to have friends at work. Enjoying social interaction is considered a positive thing in a work environment. This is true; however, it changes when an individual becomes a manager. At that point, impartiality is critical, and bias and favoritism can destroy a department or organization. Followers need to see an even playing ground. They need to trust that their efforts will be honestly assessed and valued. Connections can help expedite processes between departments, so a good working relationship is quite helpful across the organization, but in a hierarchical structure, there must be definition and delineation between managers and subordinates, leaders, and followers.

One of the most discouraging experiences for an employee is to feel that he or she is not treated fairly by his or her supervisor. The morale of an entire department or organization may suffer if employees perceive favoritism and find their own contributions diminished due to personal relationship preference. This will impact on the ability of anyone to be a good follower. I observed a great deal of bias and favoritism in my first job, and it made me particularly sensitive to even the perception of it when I became a manager. I took great pains to create a fair working environment, maintaining a professional distance between myself and my staff with no single employee having greater access than another.

At my first job, favoritism was ingrained in the culture. They considered family and personal relationships to be a strength of the company. It was considered a compliment when an employee would bring their son or daughter in to get hired. The job became generational.

I was uncomfortable with the culture of the organization because I believed in merit and earning my way to advancement. Popularity was never my strong suit so I knew if popularity outweighed merit, I would not be successful in this organization. I also knew that I would most likely strongly resent those who were promoted without merit. I was not a good cultural fit, so I was probably not a very good follower. There were many people, however, who loved working for this company. I met several people who had spent their entire career, or planned to spend their entire career, within this organization. I knew early on that I would not be one of those people.

Before I was able to leave that organization, I witnessed a situation that demonstrates the strategic importance of decision-making and the leader/follower relationship. This experience remained prevalent in my memory and often came to mind as I pursued a more advanced understanding of organizational structure and decision-making authority. As I mentioned, the manager of our department was not often available to her team. She may have had meetings with other department heads, or she may have just been socializing. I don't know what she was doing, but I do know that those of us who directly reported to her had difficulty connecting with her during our workday. Other managers were available, so we were not without leadership, but other department heads were not given the authority to make certain decisions in her absence.

Our manager required signed approval when a request came from a customer requiring an exception to normal protocol. No other manager was given this authority, as she established the process. This would normally be a very reasonable structure and process, however, with all decision-making authority under only one person, it would require that person to be consistently available. Otherwise, the sole individual can cause a bottleneck, slowing progress for the rest of the team. In this case the manager retained unilateral authority, so she was the sole person charged with this type of decision-making for the department. We often waited hours to complete a task because she would not allow anyone else to approve a special request from a customer.

One day, a woman who had worked in the department for several years by this time was trying to resolve a situation for a large and important commercial customer. As I remember it, she came up with a workable solution, had the customer's acceptance, and did as much as she could to finalize the correction and provide confirmation back to the customer but then her hands were tied as she needed approval of the decision from the supervisor to make the correction. Since this employee was experienced and had already determined the path forward, all she needed was the required, written, approval from the manager for what she recommended as the best solution for the customer. In other words, she knew what needed to be done and how to do it, but she lacked the authority to make the decision to move forward.

The employee went looking for approval from the manager, however, the manager could not be found. After what I believe was a few hours, if I remember correctly, the employee became frustrated and went ahead and took care of the customer and finalized the operation without the required approval. When the manager eventually returned to the department and the employee told her that she had made the decision without the supervisor, she was fired. At the time, I remember thinking how very wrong it seemed to terminate someone for trying to do her job when she was trying to do the right thing for the customer while hampered by, what I termed at that time, an irresponsible and absent manager.

With the benefit of many years of experience behind me and a great deal of research on the topic, I now would assess the situation as a failure of decision-making structure. The manager may have had a very good reason for requiring her authorization for every decision. It may have been a requirement handed down by her manager, or some other higher authority. It may have been standard operating procedure and an organization-wide process that no individual manager could change. The entire company seemed to be centrally organized with authoritarian decision-making so her process would be consistent with the culture and structure of the organization. She may have had very good reasons, but it simply did not work.

A centralized structure may be workable in certain environments, but not environments where the individual with the decision-making authority is not regularly accessible during working hours. In this situation, this particular structure made the department inefficient, and the employees frustrated. If the manager knew she would often be away from the department and yet customer service often demanded a quick response, she should have adapted to that reality or, if structural changes were optional, developed another structure that would have accommodated her regular absence. If it was a company-wide process, then it was time for a review of that process given the challenges of our department. The company lost a good employee unnecessarily due to a very solvable organizational deficiency.

Leaders can retain tight control, or they can delegate it, but they need a plan, and it must be consistent and thoroughly communicated, leaving employees confident in their understanding of their role. Could this supervisor not have assigned a "back-up" person for decisions? Could she not have allowed exceptions based on the critical nature of the problem and, perhaps, the potential for consequences or losses from an angry customer? If the employee strongly believes that they are at risk of losing an important account, could a process allow for documentation of the rationale behind the decision and justification to prove to the manager that he or she made a necessary decision in his or her absence? There are many ways to establish a decision-making process but retaining all authority while being inaccessible is not a recommended method.

Some might think the answer is for all employees to have equal decision-making authority. That is not the answer either. In this case, for example, if I had decision-making authority I would likely have made very bad mistakes. As a new employee with no experience, I was not prepared for that level of authority. The more senior staff, however, might have been knowledgeable and capable enough to make some decisions.

When businesses have tried to establish flat hierarchies wherein all employees make all decisions and no individual has decision-making authority, it has largely proven to be a failed system as well (Griffin, 2022). Some employees don't have the knowledge or the preparation to participate in decision-making. Some employees do not have the desire to participate in decision-making. Including many different people with multiple different opinions means a conclusion may be difficult to reach when too many people have equal authority. A final decision maker is often the only way to keep projects moving along (Griffin-Ray, 2022).

Structure determines how the work will be divided and who will have various levels of authority (Schein, 2017). The founder of an organization creates, "the need for coordination, which eventually turns into some form of hierarchy that, in turn, creates an authority structure" (Schein, 2017, p. 170). As a new organization develops, what also must be determined are the rules for power, influence, and authority. "The process of stratification in human systems is typically not as blatant as the dominance-establishing rituals of animal societies, but it is functionally equivalent in that it concerns the evolution of workable rules for managing aggression and mastery needs" (Schein, 2017, p. 170). Schein (2017) expresses a need for workable rules that can facilitate effective functioning while attempting to reduce the influence of those with an aggressive nature. When everyone is in charge, no one is in charge and conflict can paralyze an organization. What is desirable is clear, understandable, effective interaction between leader and follower.

If an organization can develop good followers, leading becomes far easier. People all need to understand the structure, the plan, and the process for decision-making. Not all employees can be leaders, but a good starting point is to work at becoming a good follower. Participant Mark also pointed out the ability to understand people and to recognize the best role in the organization for them to fit into when selecting followers and building a team. Sometimes people are just in the wrong role and that causes a problem for the leader and the department or organization. It's an important skill for leaders to select the right followers for their team when they have the choice. "The insight into people is critical. You have to be able to judge character. You have to be able to determine if these are the right people" (M. H., 2022). A leader needs to have followers who are a good fit for the organizational culture and leadership style of the leader.

  There are organizations with structures intentionally devised to develop employee growth and leadership. Amazon, for example, has created a system that structures decision-making to encourage participation of followers within certain parameters. Other decisions are clearly assigned to higher-level leaders. Amazon attempts to incorporate lower-level staff in lower risk decisions. This allows them to benefit from incorporating the ideas, information, and experience those employees can offer. Without including employees at the low end of a hierarchical structure the organization may lose valuable knowledge and, perhaps more importantly, discourage those seeking a route to upper management. This can represent a loss to a company as well in terms of ideas and innovation (McGrath, 2019). Amazon provides an example of how to strategize decision-making. Some decisions clearly are made by upper management, while some decisions invite more participation. The first lesson to take from this is that Amazon is strategic and thoughtful in how they structure and implement decision-making.

The role of followers should not be dismissed. A good follower tends to be a committed, loyal employee. While in a follower role, employees need to understand what followership entails. In today's world of sensitivity and emotion, it is not always politically correct to remind an employee that he or she is not in charge, however, it's one of the best things you can do for the organization, and for that individual. A follower is evaluated as a follower and employees labeled "uncooperative" or "not a team player" can find their career at a standstill.

Once a decision is made, a follower who refuses to implement or adhere to the direction becomes a problem for the entire organization. In a highly regulated organization, refusing to follow the directive of a leader may result in sanctions or fines affecting far more than the one individual or department. While it won't make you the most popular manager, it is critical that you enforce followership and adherence to the role.

One experience I had while managing a team exemplifies the importance of good followership. At the time, I had one employee who seemed to have a very difficult time as a follower. She may have wanted to lead, or just be disruptive, but regardless of the motivation, it was a problem for the entire organization. With this employee, we will call "Jill" I had explained several times, and mandatory training reinforced this message, that all marketing materials for public use must go through the compliance department for compliance approval. This employee was loathe to ask for approval and refused to request approval from our compliance team. Part of the problem was she was continuously behind and missed due dates for deliverables to clients. She was able to save herself some time by skipping the required compliance approval, which could delay a project for days or weeks.

    I had several discussions with Jill each time she "missed" part of the required process. She always said that she understood and promised it would not happen again. After multiple attempts at correction, I finally had to assert more authority and directly address the failure of followership and the likely outcome of someone who simply could not, or would not, comply with a serious directive. When I noticed a package addressed to one of our corporate clients waiting to be picked up by the delivery company, I went to ask Jill about the materials she was shipping. I told her I did not remember seeing the final product with the required compliance approval, yet I see it set up for delivery. I asked her very pointedly if she was sure she had compliance approval to send the materials out to be used. She assured me that she had received approval. I reminded her that I could easily check the final copy because if compliance approved it, they would have a copy in their files. She assured me that the compliance file would have the approved marketing materials. Rather than continue arguing I calmly said, "That's good because if that package leaves here without compliance approval in the file, this time it will cost you your job." She literally jumped up from her desk and ran to the reception area to retrieve that package. She started the compliance approval process and called the client to let them know that the promised deliverables would, once again, be late.

Followers have a role and a responsibility and an obligation to the leader they report to. They are expected to follow directions and be honest in their communication. Followership is important to the functioning of the entire organization. Learning to be a good follower can also help develop skills and awareness that will lead to becoming a better leader. Unfortunately, rather than encouraging good followership, people are often now applauded for obstructing authority and "resistance" has become virtuous. This current reality is probably doing more damage to organizations than we realize. I suspect we will see worse consequences in future years given what the culture has created.

Leaders and followers must work with synchronicity. There is an unspoken agreement between the leader and the follower that there is a shared responsibility, and each one is expected to fulfill their role within the organizational structure or plan. There is a mutual exchange between leader and follower. There should be an understanding of honesty and trust. Once trust is lost, it is very difficult to recover. Both leaders and followers invest in each other's success and contributions to the organization. "The transactional theorists contribute the basic idea that authority consists of reciprocal relationships; people in authority influence constituents, but constituents also influence them. We forget this at our own peril" (Heifetz, 1994, p. 19).

Leaders and followers must work together to ensure the success of the organization. A leader cannot lose sight of the importance of followers, but followers also must recognize the leader and make every effort to responsibly and ethically comply with the authority provided.

Without the capable functioning and reciprocity of the team dynamic it is very difficult to have success. The relationship between leader and follower is not always easy, and there is a give and take that occurs which sometimes can become strained. It is also a different relationship for some personality types. Some need more interaction while some prefer less. Some need autonomy while some function better with structure. Leaders will benefit when they know how to connect with each follower.

Successful leaders can generate loyalty in followers. Improving leadership skills can make it easier for followers to desire to follow and eventually build loyalty. In the next chapter we will describe two leadership styles that may be excellent models for most organizations challenged by a competitive marketplace and in an unusually fast paced, technology-driven environment.

CHAPTER SIX
AUTHENTIC AND ADAPTIVE LEADERS

There is not one way to lead. There is not one method for decision-making or one way to design organizations. There are different types of leaders and different types of organizations. Sometimes it's a matter of finding the right fit between the leader and the organization. Authentic leaders are those who are genuine. They may not have all the answers, but they are true to themselves and their values. Those who attempt to create a façade or develop a persona for the organization may have trouble once a real crisis occurs and instinct and natural leadership is what is called for. A crisis or an unusual condition can result in pulling back the curtain of corporate disguise revealing the disguise. It is best to be your authentic self from beginning to end.

Part of being a leader is being who you are (Adjibolosoo, 2018). People are beings mired in habit and social engagement. They tend to acclimate towards the social culture that surrounds them and find a comfortable space that accommodates their personality and character. People tend to resonate with the things around them that mirror who they are internally (Adjibolosoo, 2018). "Thus, regardless of the nature and intensity of external stimuli, a person's attitude, behavior, and actions are determined by what he or she is. Indeed, whatever an individual's inner person is made to be by all the factors that have shaped him or her throughout the years, it is these same factors that determine a person's whole being," (Adjibolosoo, 2018, p. 103).

We all know people we call phonies or fakes. Most of us can remember working with people we called "brown-nosers" or "butt-kissers" or some other similar name. These people often do not even realize how transparent their cowardice is to those around them. People who are disingenuous are unreliable and cannot inspire confidence in followers. Leaders lacking authenticity will discourage trust or reliance and, consequently, will be relegated to leadership through use of negative power. Those with fewer leadership skills will need to use more authoritarian power, often relying on formal position or a punishment/reward construct as opposed to those more skilled leaders who may not need to assert as much authority to accomplish the same task (Yukl, 2009).

The sycophantic hierarchical climber is bent on reaching new heights. Their growth and advancement are more important than those they manage. These people are incredibly detrimental to an organization as they are typically unreliable to the people they lead, as well as the people they follow. No one in the reporting chain can count on support because any controversy or conflict is not acceptable to the sycophant. He or she needs to "go along and get along" to be sure his or her position is secure and advancement likely. Those beneath this type of person in the hierarchy are simply the fuel to the fire of the self-important.

Leadership Styles

An authentic leader will rely on his or her own personality, traits, and beliefs to lead. An adaptive leader will adjust based on the circumstances and the individuals comprising the team. I believe that the combination of those two leadership styles may result in optimal leadership and decision-making for most organizations. While the literature suggests that the transformative leader is the ideal, there is also acknowledgement that an extremely small number of people will ever rise to the level of a transformative leader. When faced with an unachievable ideal or aspiration, leaders can become discouraged. If we were asked to name someone who we consider a transformational leader, we would probably have difficulty doing that without relying on political history. It is doubtful that any of us can recall working for a transformational leader. However, we may have worked for many very good leaders.

There are many different leadership styles, and each leader needs to feel comfortable in how he or she leads. Authenticity means a leader will be genuine with others in the organization, both up and down the hierarchy. There is no single mold that is perfect for every leader. Personality will make a difference. There are a range of personalities that can fit into a leadership role.

Leaders also need to know how their success as a leader will be measured. Achievable and realistic goals provide leaders and potential leaders with optimism about improvement in their role. Authenticity is character and behavior driven. Adaptability is a skill. Decision-making requires both honesty and flexibility, in terms of character. As new information becomes available, adaptability is key at each point where a different view of the decision is revealed. When a timeline looms large, a decision must be made within the context of reality, accepting a lack of perfection. It may not be perfect, but it will be real, genuine, authentic, and honest. That is the goal of a good leader.

Authentic Leadership

Authentic leadership has become more prominent in leadership theory in recent years and has been positioned as a strong contender for challenges facing modern leaders (Caza & Jackson, 2011). The concept of authentic leadership is evolving, but it has already proven valuable. Authentic leadership also emphasizes the moral component thus making it consistent with efforts in many business schools to develop ethical leaders. It now is used frequently by those in actual leadership roles, i.e., a practitioner as opposed to a theorist. While there is some disagreement about the definition of an authentic leader in the literature, as a pragmatist and practitioner, I will define it as I see it from a practitioner's position and from a perspective of what would be most useful for those intending to *practice* leadership, not *reflect on* leadership.

From this practitioner position, the simple understanding of an authentic leader is a person who is not afraid to be who they really are including values, principles, ethics, and morals. An authentic leader is "comfortable in his or her own skin" and not concerned with what others think. They do not seek popularity or constant affirmation. They are nonconformist and reliably committed to an ethical, and optimistic, world view.

Those interested in practicing authentic leadership must be self-aware, able to recognize and acknowledge their own values and principles, and they must be willing to be open and straightforward (Caza & Jackson, 2011). Authentic leaders should be positioned well for decision-making, relying on the foundation of authenticity and his or her own humanity. One who is, "comfortable in his or her own skin" can be truly authentic and decisions would be genuine and with clear intention. Authenticity is often intuited by others, recognized as genuine and reliable. Authentic leaders will logically be consistent in decision-making as they will use their own lens reliably regardless of the issue or situation.

> A pattern of leader behavior that draws upon and promotes both positive psychological capacities and a positive ethical climate, to foster greater self-awareness, an internalized moral perspective, balanced processing of information, and relational transparency on the part of leaders working with followers, fostering positive self-development (Walumbwa et al., 2008, p. 94).

Authentic leaders approach decision-making with a positive attitude and can-do spirit. They believe that every problem has a solution, and every issue contains at least some thread of good outcome. Decisions are considered opportunities, not drudgery or impositions. While some people avoid or hide from decisions, authentic leaders can embrace decision-making as truth seeking and integrity infusing adventures.

According to Caza and Jackson (2011), followers may benefit tremendously from working for authentic leaders. Employees may sense a more positive culture and a leader comfortable with himself or herself can be more relaxed and relatable. It is a leadership style very appropriate for current times given the need for ethical leadership as more areas of corruption are exposed in both business and government. It may be a method to counter and uproot the prevalence of corruption, greed, and the self-serving nature so often seen in business and political leaders. Many people are entirely frustrated and disgusted with the dishonesty and disengagement of many of today's self-serving leaders. Authenticity is craved in cultures infected with political ploys and manipulations.

Presuming my arguments in support of authentic leadership are compelling, you may be thinking that authentic leadership sounds optimal for your purposes, and you would like to adopt this approach. How exactly does one become an authentic leader? Bill George (2003) developed an authentic leadership approach that focuses on characteristics and qualities of the leader and ways to develop those qualities. George (2003) discovered through his research that authentic leaders demonstrate five basic characteristics.

1. They understand their purpose.
2. They have strong values about the right thing to do.
3. They establish trusting relationships with others.
4. They demonstrate self-discipline and act on their values.

5.   They are passionate about their mission.

An authentic leader may start with specific traits. They have confidence, hope, optimism, and resilience. These traits are more likely to lead to the successful development of an authentic leadership approach. They are traits because they are characteristics of an individual's personality, typically evident long before they land in a leadership role. While people born with these traits more naturally acclimate to a leadership role, some skills can be improved that help develop leaders through training and coaching (Northouse, 2016). Coaching and mentoring can guide the leader in his or her development and growth along this path.

In addition to training and coaching, critical life events can change an individual's perspective (Northouse, 2016). Challenges and difficulties build character and improve skills. Someone who can "get back up" once he or she has been "knocked down" builds resilience and hope that will last a lifetime. Critical events allow people to stretch and grow beyond their comfort zone. Change and new experiences can be invaluable to a developing leader. Some leaders stay with what's comfortable and avoid risk so as they advance within their organization, they miss the essential growth and development opportunities that can only arise through a new experience and a change in atmosphere.

One of the most unique aspects of the authentic leader is their sense of purpose and commitment to direction. This often keeps the leader moving forward, progressing, and persevering even in the face of adversity. They believe what they are doing is right and they are supposed to be where they are, doing what they are doing. For many this is grounded in faith. It is grounded in belief that God has a plan for your life and a mission for you to accomplish. Believers will function in their role the way their faith guides them. They are not swayed by the expectations of pop culture. For some, it may be grounded in natural law or other beliefs but, regardless of the source, they believe in something bigger than themselves and that gives them purpose.

Those who have a purpose and lead with values may find themselves in conflict with leaders who are more focused on some other self-serving aspects of their job. A focus on purpose and values can place one leader outside the leadership team or asserting a position not popular with the CEO. The leader choosing this path may find frustration, but the purpose is still worth fighting for. Those more driven by purpose than power will benefit the organization and the people surrounding them. According to George, (2003), when a leader pursues an authentic approach, the winners are the subordinate employees. Thus, this model is well worth pursuing.

People want leaders to be more transparent (Northouse, 2016). People would like to be able to trust their leaders, both in business and politics. "In exchange, people are willing to give leaders greater loyalty and commitment" (Northouse, 2016, p. 199). To develop a trusted relationship, leaders must communicate with followers. There must be an interactive relationship built between the leader and the staff so that employees recognize the intent of the leader even if the outcome does not seem favorable to him or her.

Authentic leadership will produce authentic decision-making. With thoughtful reflection and honesty, an authentic leader will approach a decision. He or she will still need to have a decision-making strategy, but once established, there will be no confusion about how decisions are made and what framework is used.

Authentic leadership; has an explicit moral dimension. Underlying both the practical and theoretical approaches is the idea that authenticity requires leaders to do what is "right" and "good" for their followers and society. Authentic leaders understand their own values, place followers' needs above their own, and work with followers to align their interests to create a greater common good" (Northouse, 2016, p. 207).

An employee may disagree with a decision, but he or she can be reasonably assured that the leader made the decision consistent with his own known lived experiences and moral underpinnings. Followers will, over time, recognize patterns and feel confident in consistency and the moral framework the leader is using. This brings stability and comfort to an organization, even during times of conflict, controversy, and change.

Adaptive Leadership

Adaptive leadership focuses primarily on the follower and how the leader can help the follower achieve the objective of the work

(Northouse, 2016). "The goal of adaptive leadership is to encourage people to change and learn new ways of living so that they may do well and grow" (Northouse, 2016, p. 258). The ability to adapt is crucial to environments where change occurs regularly. Many business cultures are constantly evolving and changing to deal with a competitive environment or a demanding customer. If an organization fails to adapt, they will not survive. If a leader fails to adapt, he or she will become irrelevant.

Adaptable people will remain calm and committed and persevere in the face of challenges. An adaptive leader works hard to guide staff through changes and he or she will make a serious effort to help employees be prepared for things they might encounter during times of change. Employees may experience emotional reactions, as well as practical fall-out from new processes, procedures, training, additional workloads, and operational adjustments. Adaptive leaders need to push employees out of their comfort zone so they can learn new things and become flexible and agile. Managers need to continue to challenge employees to take on new things and do things differently than they have done before. Employees will grow when they are encouraged to think about things in various ways, considering new thoughts and different ideas. Some will respond more positively than others. Some employees will embrace change and welcome a new challenge. Some will resist and reject the change, attempting to control or even undermine the efforts. Leaders may need to push harder with these reluctant or complacent employees.

Resistant employees may need to be encouraged and handheld a little to get them to move down the path of growth and change. Some will continue to cling to the familiar and comfortable. Some will advance, but more slowly. Some will rise to the challenge and be energized at the opportunity to tackle new ideas, thoughts, and actions. This, again, requires a leader to know the followers and understand their capacity, energy, and interest. A stable, solid employee may be an asset in a growth environment, or he or she may be an inhibitor of progress.

Adaptive leaders will challenge norms and not allow people to remain stagnant. He or she recognizes and acknowledges the comfort of continuity but effectively emboldens employees to think bigger and do more. He or she offers support and encouragement, lowering the fear of failure. People must be willing to fail if they are willing to take a chance to do something new. As long as we learn from our mistakes, we are still advancing in our growth and evolution.

For several years I managed a marketing department where I had a great staff with a lot of talent. There was a large amount of work in our department, and they worked hard. We had tight deadlines and always had multiple projects going on at the same time. With so many activities and projects and everyone working at a fast pace, there were bound to be mistakes. If I had created an environment where mistakes would be chastised and punished, I would have restricted creativity and each person's unique contributions and ideas. Instead, I advised my team that they should not worry about mistakes, because they were bound to happen. Mistakes that were unintentional were just mistakes that needed to be fixed. I had an agreement with them that if they would just tell me as soon as they realized there was a mistake or a problem, they had my word that all I cared about was fixing the problem. I told them the sooner they let me know, the sooner I could get busy solving it with, hopefully, fewer negative consequences. In other words, what I found was that if employees feared a bad outcome for themselves, they were more likely to hide a mistake hoping it would escape unnoticed. However, mistakes, left uncorrected, could cause many more problems with cascading issues. It was far preferable to acknowledge and admit mistakes and then work quickly to correct the problem.

  Clients and colleagues were more forgiving and understanding when we were proactive, took ownership, and attempted to make things right as quickly as possible. I had a better chance to catch a mistake if I heard about it early and responded quickly. My team was talented, hardworking, and smart. Mistakes were just mistakes. As a team, we would dive in and fix mistakes as best we could. We would learn from the mistakes but not dwell on them. There was no blame or individual finger pointing. The whole team would pull together to help fix a problem even if it meant staying late or doing additional work. As a team, we were able to correct mistakes far better than the individual employee left on his or her own.

  I was able to implement this approach because the leaders I reported to at the time understood how a marketing department functions, and they delegated enough authority for me to make decisions independently. They also trusted that I would know when it would be best for me to seek approval or request input on a decision or notify the CEO if there was a problem. With the leadership support provided to me from the level I reported to, I was able to lead effectively at my level of management. The clarity offered through the decision-making structure allowed me the best opportunity to lead effectively with my teams. I had the benefit of leadership that was de-centralized enough to allow me to manage freely, learning from the inevitable mistakes as I grew in the role.

The first CEO I worked for in a management role used mistakes as a learning tool, but he could also make it a very uncomfortable lesson. He spent a great deal of time discussing how to make sure the error did not happen again, and it was often a very unpleasant discussion. The lesson was learned, but it wasn't painless.

The second CEO I worked for created an environment where people did not fear making a mistake. He was straightforward with no hidden agendas. He made it easy to discuss issues and present alternative opinions. While he may have been frustrated, he understood that mistakes were inevitable in a busy, productive, department. He also helped correct mistakes and was supportive of being part of a solution. He offered constructive criticism to help prevent the same, or similar, problem from happening again, but he communicated in a respectful and professional manner.

I tried to empower my team similarly, although as a new manager and still learning at the time, my efforts were imperfect. Experiences lead to improvements over time. What enabled success in that environment was having a CEO who established trusted relationships with his executives and, in turn, that emphasis on trust and honesty filtered throughout the entire organization. The commitment leadership needed from staff was the expectation of honesty and openness, to whatever degree possible. Again, the trust had to go both directions and was needed up and down the organizational chart. In all areas of the operation, it was important to have staff who were willing to be humble and honest about mistakes, so leadership had the best opportunity to get ahead of the problem and mitigate the damage to protect a client or other partner. The goal was to do damage control and some quick re-positioning with clients or other stakeholders affected.

When we had a significant mistake or problem, we needed the best, most accurate, information about the situation and we needed ideas and input from anyone with relevant knowledge (Griffin-Ray, 2022). We would adapt as needed. The earliest possible warning provided an opportunity to pull together a team to share responsibility and get the work done or the issue solved. I could seek support from other department managers if needed. We all knew that it benefited the entire organization if we worked together to fix a problem. This also helped build trust and camaraderie as we came together to support the employee or team with the crisis. There were always people willing to jump in and support a teammate. They also knew that when the time came that person would reciprocate the support.

Adaptive leaders tend to use more participatory decision-making processes as they need ongoing information, and they need to be aware of changes quickly. "One produces progress on adaptive problems by working the conflicts within and between the parties" (Heifetz, 1994, p. 121). According to Heifetz (1994), decision-making and problem solving can benefit from discussion and debate between involved participants. Based on my research, I would add that the participants must also be knowledgeable, experienced, and informed on the subject. Heifetz (1994) also suggests that adaptive leaders may use a more authoritarian decision-making approach due to several factors. It may be that the followers are not up to the stress and effort involved in adaptive work. They could become overwhelmed and retreat to their comfort zone, rejecting the changing direction (Heifetz, 1994). Inability to contribute to a discussion or decision may be due to a lack of experience in challenging conversation and conflict. Employees may simply not be used to debating with the boss or expressing any disagreement with what at least appears to be the prevailing opinion.

Another concern identified by Heifetz (1994) is employees may be unable to accept "short-term pain to obtain long-term benefit" (p. 121). They may be unwilling to accept their own short-term discomfort as they simply do not envision a future for themselves or the organization. Whether by design or simply a lack of foresight, employees may be more concerned with their own here and now than with the organization's future. Subordinates may lack the understanding of the shared responsibility of those involved in the decision-making (Heifetz, 1994).

Some employees, particularly entry level staff, may not be used to, or comfortable with, working with groups or teams. The culture of the organization may not encourage teamwork or sharing of ideas and effort. Finally, and perhaps most importantly, there may not be a bond of trust between leaders and followers or within the organization. Trust is essential and yet efforts to build trust are often ignored. This is not just the responsibility of the leader; however, it is also the responsibility of the followers. Trust must be mutual with both a leader trusting his or her followers and the followers trusting their leaders. The relationship is a contract between employer and employee with negotiations and re-negotiations as both adapt while situations evolve and change.

During a crisis, Heifetz (1994) says there may simply not be enough time for any type of participatory decision-making. Autocratic decision-making may be necessary. While working to improve trust and other positive elements of decision-making, sometimes confidence in the leader is what is necessary to move a situation forward. Autocratic decision-making may be the best approach if some issues exist. Followers look to a leader, particularly in a crisis, expecting them to be decisive and determine a path forward.

An effective leader recognizes when it is time to make a quick decision and act rather than wait for input, meetings, discussions, or surveys. Heifetz (1994) offers a rule of thumb. "One becomes more autocratic-exclusive when the issue is likely to overwhelm the current resilience of the group or society given the time available for decision" (p. 122). An adaptive leader intends to be relational but must also recognize when participatory decision-making is simply not always the best method for achieving the best result. An adaptive leader can function effectively within a range of decision-making frameworks. There is skill involved in deciding when to make a decision, when to delegate a decision, and when to use a participatory model including others in your decision-making process (Griffin-Ray, 2022).

Aspiring to be Adaptive

As an adaptive leader, it is important to retain a strength of conviction tempered with an openness to another's reality. An adaptive leader will look for uniqueness in existing staff members. He or she will look for agility and adaptability when recruiting new individuals to join an existing team, department, or organization. It's important to match the individual with the job. Victor Frankl states, "man's heart is restless unless he has found, and fulfilled, meaning and purpose in life (Frankl, 1969). If people utilize the skills and talents that they have, they should find meaning. If they are in a job they do not like, or they are not successful, it is a very long, dreary life.

Frankl also provides foundation to the adaptive leadership style as he describes "unique meanings of the individual situations" (Frankl, 1969). Each person has their own individual life journey and each person's scenario, and interpretation may be entirely their own. As adaptive leaders, we are more likely to recognize that all employees have talents and traits and each response to a situation we face can be different, due to our individuality. Companies are filled with processes, plans, systems, and order but we will be remiss, as leaders, if we neglect to recognize the difference in the individual people we work with. Frankl

(1969) also says that meaning can be interpreted differently. If that's the case, we may need to consider how effective we can be as leaders if we are relying primarily on email and online communication. Leaders need to get to know people. Taking a walk around the floor affords valuable, informal interaction. Understanding the strengths and weaknesses of staff is much more likely with regular, ongoing, and direct communication.

The adaptive leadership model is specifically focused on stewarding staff through change. Some employees embrace change, and others have difficulty with it. Conflicts between those adapting to change and those clutching the safety of status quo will be better handled by leaders driven by ethics, highly skilled in communication and trained in social and emotional intelligence.

In the adaptive model, a leader "helps followers deal with conflicting values that emerge in changing work environments and social contexts. Change and learning are inherent in organizational life, and adaptive leadership focuses specifically on helping followers to confront change and examine the emergence of new values that may accompany change" (Northouse, 2016, p. 275).

Business environments are changing rapidly. The advancement of technology and automation has increased the speed of change such that there is almost always at least one new product, system, or process being trained most of the time, in most organizations. In today's environment, leaders are constantly managing through change, training new skills, and spending precious time and resources reducing the stress and anxiety that naturally arise in times of change. Adaptive leaders serving with a purpose are committed to helping employees deal with change, for themselves and the team and organization they serve. They can develop a level of comfort as they find ways to incorporate their own value system into an evolving environment (Northouse, 2000). With an adaptive ethical leader at the helm, employees may be steered through change and conflict and towards their own individual purpose and self-fulfillment. Every human being has a purpose and, if they search for it, the purpose will be revealed (Frankl, 1969). Each person needs to be willing to work at it, take responsibility, and seek meaning and a good adaptive leader would place a high priority on having employees who can finding satisfaction and purpose within the organization.

  According to Frankl, all of life is a quest for meaning (2006). Given how much time is spent at work, leaders can be instrumental in guiding followers to the quest for meaning. If an employee is very unhappy and does not seem to be effectively utilized, then a pleasant separation should be acceptable to both parties. Fear of turnover should not deter leaders from building teams of outstanding followers driven by values and integrity. When faced with making a change in employment arrangements, people often delay due to fear of the unknown. Once the change is made, it often becomes clear that the only mistake in the decision is that it took too long to make (Cloud, 2010). Employees should feel comfortable changing jobs. There is no longer a stigma attached to job changers. Most people now realize the benefit of an employee with a range of experiences. Similarly, managers need to realize when it is time to make the difficult decision to encourage an employee to leave if the role is not working as planned or the company or individual has simply grown in a separate direction. It may be that the employee is just not a good fit for the role or the organization. It maybe that it was a good arrangement for a time, but then the employee wanted to grow and that required making a change. As companies grow, they also face cultural changes. Perhaps the culture of the organization is no longer what the employee wants it to be. "But there is a time, a moment, when it is truly over, and if that is not in your view of life, you can miss the right time to get out and to turn your attention to something different or new" (Cloud, 2010, p. 40).

In some cases, managers are faced with employees who are just difficult to manage. Followers who refuse to follow will, one way or another, cause problems. The amount of time and energy a manager can spend on one disruptive or difficult employee costs the entire department or organization. Time is better spent developing the willing, than coercing the resistant.

While managing a training department, I established an employee development program. This program became popular as word spread that the class was very honest and transparent about career aspirations, even when those aspirations would clearly lead to a path other than what one could find within the organization. Most organizations are averse to encouraging good employees to seek opportunities that would require them to leave the company, but the truth for some was simply that they had other dreams that could not be met within our organization. Rather than stumbling through a frustrating career, helping employees find a better fit seemed like a worthwhile endeavor.

One employee in my career pathing class went through the entire one-year program and, at the end, gave her final presentation which was an assignment for each participant to present their vision for their future ideal career. This young woman went to the front of the class for her presentation, and she shared what she has recognized to be her true passion. She decided that her ambition was to be a "domestic engineer", as she called it. Her goal was to have children and be a stay-at-home Mom. This was not the expected outcome of a corporate employee career pathing program, but it was obvious to all of us that she had discovered what would bring meaning to her life. The program and the process of self-reflection had revealed that to her. It took courage, and trust, to share in front of a group of co-workers that her career goal was to leave her career. Her presentation was honest, authentic, and powerful. She clearly spoke from the heart. At the end of her presentation, there was enthusiastic applause, and a few tears.

Adaptive Power

An effective adaptive leader will need to reject the temptation to misuse power. Leaders should use power and authority to stand up for the right thing and support what is good and what is decent and against corruption or injustice. A good adaptive leader will also make efforts to allow other voices to be heard (Northouse, 2016). Sometimes, the more rational perspective is buried by the loudest voices. The quiet, the introverted, and the humble retreat in silence when pride rears its head, and the egocentrics overpower the room. Without opposition, the aggressive, loud, power will only be encouraged to advance with his or her agenda, regardless of the needs, wants, or opinions of others. A good leader should not stand aside and allow a wrongheaded decision or a biased agenda to go unchallenged just because the one presenting it is the loudest or most forceful. While we may not always win the fight, we owe it to those we lead to at least walk onto the battlefield.

As business continues to be challenged with competitive threats and technological advancement, one thing that is certain is that change will be rapid and the need for employee training and development crucial. No component of leadership will be more valuable than the ability to manage employees through change, while minimizing conflict and controversy. The adaptive leadership style is the most focused in this area and the most likely to have success managing change with grace and purpose. The adaptive style of leadership offers a sound solution to the problem of conflict while offering an environment where employees are encouraged to contribute. A leader skilled enough with this approach will add value, not only to the organization, but to the individuals who work there. The salary will become a less significant aspect of the benefits package in an organization that offers an adaptive leadership style, an ethical environment, and the opportunity to seek purpose in the work.

As employees find appreciation for their efforts and satisfaction in what they produce or how they perform, they will know they have been afforded an exceptional opportunity. While conflict will never completely disappear, perhaps the rhetoric can contain a little more civility when people feel purposeful. The other ingredient necessary to build a positive organizational culture is an emphasis on ethics and character. We cover the importance of ethics and purpose in the following chapter.

CHAPTER SEVEN
PURPOSE, ETHICS, AND INTENTIONS

Numerous books and articles have been written about ethical leaders and the importance of ethical leadership in the last few years. Business schools have attempted to implement an ethical component to their programs. Many industries and organizations train business ethics within their organizations, often making ethics training mandatory for all employees. Regardless of the renewed emphasis on ethics and attention given the issue, there still seems to be no shortage of unethical activity across the spectrum of industries and organizations. While there is a great deal more virtue signaling these days, there is far less actual virtue.

Even when individual leaders appear to be virtuous, it is often at no cost to themselves. The company allocates money to causes and the corporate leaders accept accolades. CEOs can donate to a cause, offer volunteers for an event, offer aid to a non-profit, and claim credit for the contributions when the actual sacrifice is at the expense of the organization, not the individual. It is always easier to spend other people's money, as they say. The appropriated virtue should surprise no one as the roadmap to this behavior is well worn by government. Elected officials routinely take credit for rescues, bailouts, assistance, and programs all at taxpayer expense. Rarely is the true benefactor, the American taxpayer, ever mentioned.

When assessing leadership strengths and abilities, the character issue remains critical. Determining to follow a leader can be rooted in one's own principles and adherence to ethics. In order to live, and work, according to an ethical standard, it is far preferable to report to a leader who chooses the same path. An ethical leader will create an environment and develop a culture conducive to those desiring to live according to ethical principles. If we can recognize the type of leader we are dealing with, it can make a significant difference in the progression of our career, and the serenity of our spirit. Early career experiences are also likely to impact our own ethical development. We can be affected just through exposure to our manager or mentor. That can be positive or negative, again, depending on the character and quality of the leader. Seeking to follow leaders of character can only improve our ability to become more ethical leaders once we move into that role.

While there are leaders rooted in principles and determined to honor their higher authority there are also leaders eagerly willing to ransom any individual or entity for the benefit of his or her own greed, ambition, or need for power and prestige. If you are a person hoping to grow in your organization and advance to leadership, it is very useful to have good insight into the person you report to. A person driven by a higher authority is more likely to look beyond his or herself, seeking to do what faith would dictate. On the other hand, a person who is more highly motivated by power and money will often make decisions that can become detrimental to the organization. This prioritization of self can also damage followers within the organization. A decision is likely to be made with one clear perspective, simply whether or not the outcome enhances his or her own position or finances. Knowing the character and the belief system of the person you report to is helpful as you navigate the relationship. You can often predict how a person will react to a situation if you know their character. Each individual must decide if he or she can live according to his or her value system and still be successful reporting to the boss and succeeding within the organization. If the sacrifice for success is character, it may be time to seek other employment opportunities.

Those seeking to become leaders should become very self-aware. Introspection is important for leaders. Often, we are immersed in our work we often fail to see our own flaws. We make quick decisions, rather than good decisions, and we neglect the people we are expected to lead. We are human and thus imperfect. However, if we are driven to become better leaders and to make better decisions we can work on improvements, and a critical area of focus is ethics and commitment to ethical principles. Improving in this area requires conscious, and consistent, effort.

Consider the strengthening of moral fibers as you would the process of strengthening muscles. It takes using those muscles over and over regardless of time constraints and other distractors. Virtue is acquired by habit (Aristotle, 1985). It requires sacrifice to exercise the muscle when it would be so much easier to sit and watch television. A commitment to a virtuous life means making sacrifices and being willing to be consistent in your behavior for yourself, and for those you lead. It may require standing up to those more powerful, speaking out against the current organizational, or societal culture, and then accepting the consequences of that stand. "Hence, clearly, complete virtue depends both on decision and on actions" (Aristotle, 1985, p. 288).

Interviewee Mark emphasized the importance of ethics and the responsibility of a leader to do the right thing regardless of the consequences.

"It's kind of lonely in a leadership role because everybody is taking shots at what you're doing and how you're doing it, but if you really believe it's the right thing to do and it's the right vision, then just do it. Those people, (ethical leaders) just do it. If you become unpopular, then you are unpopular" (M. H., 2022).

While the principled leader focusing on ethics and integrity may not always be the most popular person in an organization, those leading with a set of values and principles can rest more comfortably at the end of each workday and ultimately at the end of a career.

Interviewee Steve agreed that ethics are very important even when it means the outcome may not be popular or positive for some people.

I am frequently looking for the best outcome for as broad an audience as possible but I'm also trying to make sure that we're doing the right thing. And that might not be popular. That may have negative consequences for a lot of people when you do the right thing. When you stand up, when you have courage and say,

'Is this the right thing?' I do think there's an ethical framework of what's right (S.S., 2022).

Steve said leadership definitely takes courage. A good leader must be willing to go against the grain and take the time to consider the impact a decision will have. "It's not always black and white. Sometimes it's more gray. You're looking at the best outcome that affects the most people beneficially" (S.S., 2022).

Anyone leading an organization or department knows that doing what's right is often not easy. The "right" route is not always obvious either. There are hidden agendas and people skilled in manipulation. There are people who appear to be ethical, and some even hide behind religion, but eventually their true nature will be revealed. Sometimes to achieve the best outcome, more reflection and more time given to consider situations and issues can be essential. Many busy leaders often feel pressured to make decisions quickly when more time would allow for a better analysis particularly considering many potential outcomes and the varied stakeholder impacts. Steve said time is definitely important when trying to make decisions, particularly if your goal is to do what is the right thing for most people. There are decisions made that may have been made very differently with the benefit of time. Steve identifies this as a challenge particularly for newer managers. An inexperienced manager may easily feel pressured to react quickly rather than taking the time to assess the potential impact for the wide-ranging stakeholders.

> Early in your career you think you have to make the decision quicker than you probably need to. There's probably more room to consult with others to make the best decision possible. Early on you want to have a quick impact to want to show that you're decisive. All those things that make you want to be a good manager leads you sometimes to make decisions quicker than you really need to (S.S., 2022).

Steve explained the value of courage and clarity. There are times where doing what is right may also be doing what is counter to the political environment or culture. A leader may have to be the bearer of bad news, particularly if it's a decision that will have negative consequences for some. "Everyone is not going to be happy with you. I think sometimes just being honest with people and telling people despite what they want, that's just not possible. Our requirements aren't going to change. That's just the way it is. Just be frank with folks" (S. S., 2022).

Mark said the ethical component to leadership will drive better decisions and outcomes beneficial to the organization and the individual players. He said that he used an ethical framework in his various leadership roles. "I think I made decisions from an ethical framework. I remember making some decisions where I just relied on how I was raised. Based on my ethics and how I was raised that's how I knew the right thing to do and that was my framework" (M. H.., 2022).

Another strong influence on leadership development may be involvement in sports. Particularly in team sports people need to learn how to work together. Each person has an individual role, yet they are contributing the one universal effort. Mark attributed some of his leadership skills to his time playing sports. He played multiple sports throughout his youth and eventually earned a full ride scholarship to play football at Stanford University. Playing teams sports provides many lessons applicable in leadership such as structure, organization, teamwork, collaboration and coordination, good sportsmanship, humility, and many others. "I would say my experience in athletics definitely helped me develop my leadership skills. I was involved in a lot of teams, and I was a leader on many of those teams. I rely frequently on that experience" (M.H., 2022).

Mark said it was really the combination of how he was raised as a person and how he was trained as an athlete and as a leader in his athletic career that helped develop strong leadership skills and character at a young age. "I think I was always just looking for what is right. It's how I was raised, and I know a lot of that comes from my experience in athletics. Being a leader of teams was a very big part of my experience. I relied on that a lot" (M. H., 2022).

The world of sports tends to produce leaders. Pat Williams, the senior vice president of the NBA basketball team, the Orlando Magic, has shared his philosophy of leadership and his belief in the importance of ethics and doing the right thing. Williams (2010) says it is important for a leader to be honest and fair with their followers. "Wise leaders do not lie, manipulate, or take advantage of the people they lead. Rather, they inspire their followers to work together to achieve grand visionary goals" (Williams, 2010 p. 45).

Williams (2010) says that while atheists and agnostics could possibly have the same traits as people of faith, it is the belief in God that tends to influence leaders towards consistently principled behavior.

> But faith in God, by its very nature, places a demand on the believer's life. People of faith believe that God expects them to live moral and ethical lives. They seek to obey the Ten Commandments and the Golden Rule and to serve others – not merely because they believe they will one day have to account to God but also because the more they follow God's ways, the more they see that the knows what he's doing, (Williams, 2010, p. 127).

Williams (2010), says leaders accomplish great things when they motivate their followers. People of faith are often motivated by knowing they are pursuing the purpose that their maker intended for them. If each member of a team is fulfilling their purpose, the leader needs to determine the path, lead the way, and light the fire of followers. "It comes down to you," Mark said. "To your belief in God. To know what is right. I think I apply that to pretty much every problem" (M. H., 2022).

Purpose, Meaning and Morality

In a competitive marketplace, many companies feel forced to focus on production, profitability, and efficiency as opposed to principles and ethics, however this does not have to be the case. Particularly, in an industry where survival largely depends on being better than the competition, if leaders and followers are driven by purpose and the same moral compass, they can more easily all be rowing in the same direction. A well run, ethical organization can be profitable while still functioning for the benefit of the overall organization, its customers, and its employees. If all leadership team participants are ethically driven, working together collaboratively becomes far easier.

In our current society however, atheism grows, and faith is more frequently pushed out of the corporate culture. Any leadership team will likely include people with different perspectives and philosophies. Some participants will bring underlying agendas and issues. Not everyone is guided by a moral compass. Team leaders may have different goals, priorities, or plans. Some people, due to personal circumstances or economic needs, will function outside of his or her character as a means of survival. A person of character may be tempted into behavior inconsistent with his or her values because of pressure from managers, pressure from customers, or board members. A person trying to do the right thing may find insurmountable opposition when faced with a group decision and overbearing power brokers. Should we sacrifice our job to take a stand when we know resistance is futile? Each person must make that decision. Sometimes it is a matter of picking your battles and being strategic in slowly influencing the ethics of the organization. Sometimes the way the organization functions is simply unacceptable to those who are trying to live their lives within a moral framework. Then it may be time to seek other opportunities.

When a leader is overwhelmed by his or her own self-interest, the drive for power and control may overcome organizational needs causing the leader to disregard the customers, the employees, and the long-term role of the organization. The power-driven leader seeks primarily to enrich and empower himself or herself. This leader may be lacking an effective moral compass, and the absence of principles will create problems. The presence of an unethical leader can result in conflict, disappointment, dishonesty, and manipulation. The presence of one unethical leader can create challenges in building effective teams and collaborative cross-departmental projects.

Viktor Frankl (1969) explains that to be a real person, people toil, not just for themselves, but for the greater good, the family, the community, the organization, the country. He explains why people are designed to work and why there is so much meaning in that effort. He poses the question and provides the answer. "What am I if I do it for my own sake only… In no event a truly human being" (Frankl, 1969, p. 37). When leaders are motivated by meaning and purpose, a healthy, prosperous team of workers can become an integrated community.

Employees are drawn together by corporate history and culture, as well as shared experiences; both personal and professional. We work with, and for, each other and we learn, with, and for, each other. This can be the essence of business. The purpose of coming to work is much more than just completing projects and tasks. It is to work together to achieve goals and advance the mission of the organization. This is what so many organizations claim that they strive for, yet teamwork and collaboration continue to be cited as a challenge in many organizations, and in some cases, seems to be getting worse. Conflict persists, even to the point of incivility in many workplaces, not to mention public spaces.

The foundational culture of conflict may be driven by unethical leaders and the habits they form. Without a set of principles or foundation of faith, what is there to prohibit behavior that may damage the organization or hurt another employee? If one does not believe in the golden rule, what is it that would encourage a person to, "do unto others as you would have them do unto you?"

The believer rises each morning with a purpose. We seek to be instrumental in the lives of our followers. It is our purpose and commitment to the work of our maker that drives us to complete our tasks and feel satisfied at the end of the workday or a work week. It doesn't mean we are not focused on the work itself, but we do it with a sense of how it might relate to our larger destiny. Frankl lets us know that that life cannot be meaningless unless we are too lazy to seek the self we are destined to be. "Man is responsible for giving the right answer to a question, for finding the true meaning of a situation. And meaning is something to be found rather than be given, discovered rather than invented" (Frankl, 1969, p. 43). Frankl gives us no excuse for not finding meaning. It is not for others to assign it to us. It is not going to land on our doorstep if we sit at home complacently. We have free will and that free will should fuel our own drive to find answers, solutions, and understanding.

Frankl tells us it is our responsibility to find meaning in life and to find religion by our own choice (Frankl, 2000). Again, we are advised of our own free will and the importance of what we do with that will, even as it relates to religion. "We have said that religion is genuine only where it is existential, where man is not somehow driven to it, but commits himself to it by freely choosing to be religious" (Frankl, 2000, p. 77). Frankl advises, "the will to power and what one might call a will to pleasure are substitutes for a frustrated will to meaning" (Frankl, 2000, p. 89).

We are all driven to work, to produce, to create, to serve. Those who are lazy and unmotivated rarely accomplish anything. Particularly in current society, there is a growing subset of our population in the United States who seem to believe that they should not have to work but that they should be provided with compensation and rewards just to exist. This is not acceptable to principled people.

In leadership, we need to go beyond finding our own individual purpose. Leaders have a role encouraging others to find their purpose also. While each person must do the work for themselves, organizational leaders may be able to create interest and awareness just by letting employees know that they should be looking for meaning and they should feel comfortable discussing career goals and ideas with their manager.

One of the beneficial things the millennial generation brought to the workplace is acceptance of the need for purpose and a work and life balance. Earlier generations were just expected to work and keep their personal life separate. The paycheck was their purpose. Millennials refused to accept that, and thankfully when they used the weight of their numbers to influence employers, employers listened. Now, there is an easier path to address purpose and an acceptance that, as leaders, we are integral to the life and purpose of our followers. That role is essential and enduring. In the words of Frankl, "life not only holds a meaning, a unique meaning, for each and every man, but also never ceases to hold such a meaning-retaining it literally up to the last moment, to one's last breath" Frankl, 2000, p. 122).

As previously discussed, the adaptive leadership approach lends itself well to leading with purpose. Adaptive leaders provide an environment for all employees to, "learn, grow, and work on the changes that are needed" (Northouse, 2016, p. 275). As explained previously, but it bears repeating in this context, this type of leadership style involves a strong leader to follower relationship. The leader must develop trust with the follower so that he or she can help guide the follower to take on challenges and find the best place to apply their skills and abilities. The emphasis on trust is an indicator of the importance of ethics in leadership. Followers need to believe that the leader is doing the right thing. When times change, uncertainty occurs. Those who have built trust will be better positioned to lead teams through challenging and often emotional times.

As the demand for increasing speed of response, the purpose of work and the goal of building an ethical organization can get pushed to the back burner. Even a seasoned, skilled, principled leader may struggle with the pace of change and the varied rate of adaptation for each employee. Leaders focused on successfully stewarding staff can be blindsided by the stealth egocentrism of a leader driven by their need for power and control. Particularly during times of change, often a power vacuum will occur and that is when a person with an individual agenda may move swiftly and surreptitiously to overwhelm the interests of the group. Times of change present opportunities for ill-willed people to engage in corruption, hidden power and manipulation. When change occurs, it is important to be aware of agendas and to notice the evolution of the organizational culture.

Organizational Culture

A leader interested in improving the ethics of the organizational environment would build a culture with a high level of respect and courtesy. The leader would hold a high standard of integrity. Honesty would be standard, and everyone would be expected to be forthcoming and straightforward with no fear of retribution. It is a culture where people would not be attacked for expressing an opinion, even if it is not consistent with the group opinion. Disagreement and diversity of opinions and ideas can be managed within an environment of respect and openness. The standard should be set and withheld at all levels of the organization. Professional disagreement is tolerated as long as it is handled respectfully and without animosity. Disagreement should be based on facts, and it should not deteriorate into hostility.

In many organizations, a large amount of time is wasted dealing with petty arguments, complaints, and disagreements that get blown out of proportion. Much of that could be eliminated if leaders held standards and demonstrated behaviors as described above. Improvement in civility, common courtesy, and respect could quickly pay dividends. If leaders set standards and serve as role models they can guide employees to a more quality culture. Most employees would be grateful to work in an environment where unfriendly conflicts are minimized, but discussion and debate are encouraged. Most would prefer to avoid companies where fear, coercion, and arrogance rule. People who strive to place ethics at the forefront of their life are not going to be as easily manipulated into a self-serving agenda.

Sometimes when an employee is not performing well on the job, or creating drama or chaos, it is due to a deeper problem. It may have nothing to do with the job. Most of us have met people that we think just seem unhappy. If a person is happy in their personal life with solid, caring relationships, it seems likely that he or she is naturally optimistic, hopeful, and more fulfilled. Conversely, a person without significant personal relationships and other sources of personal joy may have this unhappiness seep into their day-to-day functioning on the job. This may give us insight surrounding negativity, complaining, and the conflicts that occur in most organizations every day. Sometimes it's not just that an employee hates his jobs, he hates his life.

Turnover is an annoying expense for many organizations, and it frustrates managers, but often employees leave for personal reasons, family issues, or emotional responses. An employee leaves to follow a spouse to a new location for a preferable job. A working mother decides to stay home to raise children. A dedicated son or daughter leaves a job to take care of elderly parents. Some people come to realize the value of family and relationships and choose that over a career. They will be driven by dedication and the very strong emotion of love for a family member. Job satisfaction simply cannot compete with personal joy. It is very difficult to motivate an employee to work harder when they are concerned about a person that they love. A parent may feel the need to be with a child and that draw cannot compete with a raise or promotion. Leaders should recognize the personal needs of their employees and work with them for the best outcome.

Positive relationships are very important for happiness (Haidt, 2006). Happily married people tend to be more optimistic. Connections to other people, and to God, are important, according to Haidt (2006). Religious people tend to be happier than those who do not practice any religion. Haidt says this is partially because of the relationships developed within the religious community and due to the connection to, "something beyond the self" (p. 88). The amount of money a person makes does not significantly influence the individual's level of happiness. Consequently, if an employee is unhappy at work, it may have nothing to do with the job. A higher salary or better benefits may not result in a happier employee if his or her personal life is lacking.

Often, we become immersed in the ongoing goal of retention. While organizations expect retention, sometimes it comes at such a cost that it should not even be attempted. Convincing an employee to stay with a larger salary, a promotion, or better perks may look like success in the organizational metrics, but it may be a devastating loss to that employee. They may stay on the job but never focus on the real cause of their unhappiness. Leaders who are concerned with purpose, for themselves and their followers will consider the bigger picture for the individual and not simply serve themselves with the easiest answer.

Conflict, Chaos, and Change

Most conflicts, particularly amongst leaders, are caused by power struggles and ego. Leaders tend to be competitive people by nature so it is entirely predictable that they will compete with one another within an organization. Rather than forming a leadership team, they form a leadership competition. People can choose to help or harm. Conflicts arise at work because of egos and inflated importance. With that as the instigator, harm is the likely outcome. One person sees himself as more important than others and he achieves his position in the organization by inflating his own success at the expense of others. The authoritarian leader, driven by the desire for power, is destructive of the work community and any subgroup or team.

Ferch (2012) provides a positive path to power. If power is corralled effectively, it is not always harmful. Ferch (2012) asserts that power can fight evil and stand in solidarity with the light. If channeled correctly or applied in balance with other concerns, power can be a motivator, not an oppressor. Power can be used in a positive way. "Power then is not only the power to forgive, but the power to evoke in others the tenacity to respond to darkness with light, to respond to evil with good, and to respond to hatred with love" (Ferch, 2012, p. 7). In many business scenarios, however, those with power seem to need to demonstrate that power to satisfy their own personal quest for power, regardless of the purpose. The ability to influence feeds the ego and sense of self-importance. In business, just like in politics, the allure of power can be so strong that participants become driven only by the need to retain that power. Positive influence can be employed for the good, but too often it is misused by those who do not focus on choosing to do what is right (Ferch, 2012).

In Times of Chaos

With many organizations there are conflicts that arise due to changes and the chaos that change creates. There are those who fear change and those who simply cannot function in a chaotic environment. Many people prefer consistency and the comfort of familiarity. These people conflict with the segment of the organization pushing for improvements, growth, and ongoing adaptations to the market, the competition, and the industry pressures. This produces anger and frustration among team members. When leaders are split along these lines as well the problem rages up and down the hierarchy. Biases are present, and the various unique visions shade the perspectives of the participants, making it difficult to come to any common understanding.

Departments can often function in silos during times of change. Departments have pride amongst themselves but criticize and attack other teams within their own organization. When a change is taking place, often coordination is critical, yet not all organizations have developed working relationships between departments or groups. Conflicts are common, but what role does leadership play when the disputes are internal between different departments? During times of chaos, it is critical for a leader to be present and available. He or she needs to be prepared to guide employees through the changes and the ambiguity. A leader should be prepared for emotional reactions, as well as practical fall-out from new training, additional workloads, and operational adaptations. Employees will be fearful of losing their job, and possibly fearful of gaining a different role. A skilled leader will strive to bring together the various teams and departments to try to ensure that each individual is aware of their value. They need to be reassured, with honesty and accuracy, that the role they play in the organization is significant and recognized by those in leadership roles. They need to be reminded more often than usual that they are doing a good job when they are genuinely doing a good job. If they are no longer valuable to the organization, an honest and open conversation may need to take place. Leaving the employee to wonder and worry is unfair. What they don't know leaves room for confusion, concern, and disinformation.

Typically, those who believe in a higher power are able to look beyond their own self-interest while those lacking a foundation of faith may not. Those who can look beyond themselves are far more likely to make decisions in the best interest of the most relevant individuals.

A moral leader is a role model for everyone in the organization. By your example, you teach your followers how to treat others, how to treat your customers, and even how to treat you-the leader-with proper respect. When your people see you "walk the talk" they will be inspired to emulate your moral leadership. They will make better decisions, rooted in moral principles, because they will learn moral decision making from you. Nothing undermines respect for leadership more quickly than a leader's hypocrisy. And another cements respect for leadership more firmly than a leader's integrity (Williams, 2010, p. 54).

In the next chapter we will address some of the issues surrounding the training of leaders. Can leaders be trained? If much of what is needed for leadership are traits, how do we train skills and, if we do train for skills, is that enough to develop successful leaders?

CHAPTER EIGHT
TRAINING LEADERS

Many organizations attempt to provide leadership training for their new or potential future leaders. Unfortunately, this training is often inadequate. There are several reasons for this. In this chapter we will discuss current training, what does and does not have an impact on leaders, and what organizations can do to improve the quality of their training programs.

Leadership development is often confused with manager training, and the focus can be more operational than it should be. While there is some overlap, leadership development requires a higher order of skills (Day, 2000). Leadership involves cognitive functioning, analysis and problem solving for occurrences that are not planned or predicted. "A leadership development approach is oriented toward building capacity in anticipation of unforeseen challenges" (Day, 2000, p. 582). Leadership development is expanding the thought process and flexibility of thought in the individual. Cognitive agility is a critical capacity for leaders in a fast-paced competitive market. One must be able to think and adapt to the environment and evolve as each new piece of information is revealed. You can already see why this will be much more complicated than manager training which tends to be focused on operations, processes, and basic personnel functions. It is much easier to teach management than it is to teach leadership.

Organizations interested in building leaders must look at both the individuals and then the structure. There is a difference between building leaders and developing organizational leadership (Day, 2011). According to Day (2011), both types of training are often treated the same or integrated, but they are two distinct programs. One is building individual skills and capabilities, and the other is a process of building teams and organizational effectiveness (Day, 2011). Companies interested in expanding their overall leadership capacity need to look at both the team and the individual. This is often a place where leadership training fails. As the two types of training are often considered interchangeable, the importance and significance of the difference is disregarded. We will consider both the individual as well as the team development.

Leadership development can be a costly endeavor, but not having good leaders can be far more expensive. Some companies think they are developing leaders, and they invest training dollars, however, the training may not have the impact they are hoping it will have. For most organizations, a skilled and competent leadership team is the difference between basic survival and success.

Creating a Leadership Team

A leadership team is typically comprised of division or department leaders across an organization. Some companies select specific individuals to consciously create a leadership group likely to provide vision focused on creative problem solving and decision making. Others allow the randomness of their departmental function to dictate the identity as leader. The most senior person within a department or function is automatically the leadership participant representing that group. The random approach is often where a place of weakness within the structure will occur.

Companies can benefit from strategically selecting leaders to lead the organization, but often the leadership skill is buried under the operational need. An outstanding operations manager or successful sales director may become part of the leadership team simply by virtue of their place in the organizational hierarchy. They are not selected because of their leadership skills or potential to become leaders. They may be selected because of the success they have had in their operational, or management, role. That success does not guarantee leadership success. Unskilled people promoted into leadership in this manner arrive at the leadership table without being vetted for the optimal skills and traits required of successful leaders. Often, they do not have the cognitive flexibility to fill an organizational leadership role. They may not have the strategic vision required of a leader and the interest or ability to take the macro view of the organization. Immersed in their own occupation, operation, or department, they view their place at the table as a position for advocacy, not contribution.

This type of team is often evidenced by a lack of unity of purpose and vision. This team may create a culture of antagonism and undermining as the team participants are not leaders at all but individuals filling a slot on the organizational chart. Individuals lacking organizational vision or purpose will not emerge from their own silo to contribute to the strategic growth, advancement, and problem-solving organizations require.

An organization seeking to develop a team of leaders must first require that all participants be skilled in their role as an individual leader. They need the traits, skills, abilities, decisiveness, and moral fiber discussed in other parts of this book. While it's unlikely that the organization will have a full team of highly skilled transformational leaders, the best effort should be made to find those with the best leadership skills given the talent pool within the organization. First you need the right individuals, then you build the team. According to Day (2011), "developing leaders at all organizational levels is an effective means of transforming organizations" (p. 38).

There are many ways to create opportunities to include managers with critical skills and knowledge, but the leadership team is an entity with its own purpose, and it must be treated that way. The organization will be reflective of the quality of the leadership team. The team must work together to drive towards a unified vision. "As leaders move up an organization's hierarchy, there is a need to move from an individual to relational and then collective identity" (Lord & Hall, 2005). The "collective identity" is the leadership team culture. Many organizations miss this critical part of the organizational development process.

A leadership team will have its own culture and style. The culture of the team develops based on the construction of the team and the contribution of its members. Leaders have different styles, and one may not be better than the other, but one may certainly be more suitable than another for a particular group or organization. For example, the military selects and builds leaders. The military is known for developing leaders and highly successful ones. Leaders coming from that culture, however, are not always a great fit for some other types of environments regardless of their individual skill. They may not adapt to certain industries or cultures.

An outstanding leader may still find himself or herself feeling less competent within a team that has a different leadership style or culture than what he or she is used to. This does not make them less of a leader, but simply not a fit for a particular leadership team. Leaders coming from a non-profit, for example, may perform an outstanding service in the non-profit environment, but may not easily transition into a profit-driven organization. Leadership culture is a factor that cannot be ignored when training leaders and building a leadership team. Ideally, organizations should invest in the type of person who is likely to be both an excellent individual leader and a fit for the leadership team.

One of the current trends is to rely on consultants or external programs through an outside vendor. That can leave gaps in things like culture, industry, informal leadership, organizational history, and organizational politics. If the expectation of an organization is that there is a group of senior leaders responsible for the success of the organization, then that team holds the future of that organization in their hands. The team needs to be unified in their understanding of the culture and history as well as their view of the future. The team must function effectively to gain the benefit of each leader's contribution. If the team is not cohesive or members of the team do not have trusting communication, the team will fail, and individual leaders will be rendered ineffective.

Individual Development

Training an individual to be a leader is a long-term commitment. There are plenty of programs boasting of training lasting weeks or months, but effective leadership development is a process that takes place during the course of an entire career (Day, 2011). The approach by Day et al. (2009) emphasizes the notion of a training continuum. "Leadership development is a lifelong journey that is part of an ongoing adult development process" (p. 39). Leaders confront challenges, adapt to a changing environment, and seek knowledge always. Clearly, a one-week, or even one-year course is not sufficient for leadership training. The lifelong learner seeks to improve, consistently requests feedback, and engages in personal reflection. Successful leaders are always advancing their positions and expanding their cognitive capacities. They are people with an expansive worldview and extensive, and broad, experiences. Healthy adult development is correlated with successful leadership development (Day, 2011). Those aspiring to leadership should be life-long learners who continually engage in new experiences and career expansion.

It is generally accepted that successful leadership development must include a component of real on-the-job experience (Day, 2011). Real world experience is the most effective way to develop a leader (Day, 2011). A classroom program or seminar format alone simply does not work for thorough leadership training. It should be much more in-depth and ongoing throughout the individual's career. Concepts can be introduced, and a plan created, in a classroom environment, but the actual development process will continue well beyond an initial seminar. Due to the time commitment and extensive investment, leadership development training is overwhelming, and so often unsuccessful in organizations. Organizations intending to build leaders need to devote themselves to a thorough development program or recognize that they do not have the capacity for it. If it is not something feasible for an organization, the focus should then be on recruiting talented leaders who come already skilled and do not need to be trained. Too many organizations take a person with no experience, no proven skills, and put them in a typical leadership development program for a few weeks or months and then expect them to perform. This is very misguided.

Hiring a skilled leader with training from a previous organization is the next best option for those who do not believe they have the time, resources, or personnel to train, build, and mentor leaders. Those that do decide to develop their own leaders will need to make a serious commitment including multiple training tactics, certainly real-world application, and follow through. Once an organization has a team of seasoned, experienced, talented leaders, they can be engaged to develop the next generation of leadership potential.

One of the key tactics included in thorough training is mentorship. Individuals growing into leadership roles can benefit greatly from having an excellent leader/mentor. Ongoing feedback is a critical component of education and learning (Day, 2011). A mentor can provide the critical ongoing feedback and continued guidance needed for a new leader. Experiencing multiple leaders and leadership styles can help guide a new leader as he or she develops a style and system that is authentic and successful. Having worked for multiple managers and various companies can significantly broaden the worldview as potential leaders grow and advance.

A leader trainee should be provided with opportunities to test his or her leadership abilities and then immediately scheduled for a debrief with their leadership mentor. Challenging job assignments or projects can give the trainee experience without causing damage to the company or the trainee's self-esteem if it is done under the closetful supervision of a mentor. Each success can build confidence leading to the next challenge. Mistakes or missteps are learning opportunities. Classroom experience in addition to on-the-job training and regular, ongoing, feedback from a mentor can provide a successful plan for leadership development.

I asked our participants about the type of training they received when they first entered a leadership or management role. I asked how effective the training was for them, and I asked them if they would recommend the type of training they received or something else for current trainees. All four participants had extensive training that they credited, at least partially, for their success. All participants were provided thorough training through their employer.

> I started in management with a training program at (Company name). It was a one-year program and very extensive training. I worked for various managers so I would see different management styles and decision-making styles. I got to see the whole operation. It was excellent training. It was the foundation of the career I had for 47 years," (M.C., 2022).

Participant Mark also had extensive training that he was grateful to have received at the beginning of his career.

> Yes, I was very fortunate because I had a management training program right out of college through a savings and loan in San Diego that was growing really rapidly. They had a formal management training program. Formal management training programs at that time were common in the industry. I can remember the time they brought in Ken Blanchard. Very early in the program - right at the very beginning. He had just written <u>The One-Minute Manager</u>. We actually had a small group, so it wasn't like a big group where people could get lost. He came in and did a seminar just for our small group. We had 15 or 20 in our workshop. Management involved lots of other speakers too. We had one who wrote the book on negotiations. So, I was very

fortunate to have in-depth formal training on management and leadership, (M.H., 2022).

Participant Harold also said he had excellent training prior to becoming a manager. "(Company name) provided us with tons of training. (The company) was very good about training. There was a long list of training courses for managers. I felt well prepared for the management role," (H.G. 2022).

Harold also said he also learned a great deal about management through his experiences on the job and reporting to different managers throughout his career. He said in addition to formal training, it's really important to learn through on -the-job opportunities. "It's much more important to learn on the job because it is real world and you have to actually do things, make things happen, and be responsible for the outcome," (H.G., 2022).

Harold also shared an experience where training was not effective. Although he received excellent training in the Navy, he was accidentally trained for the wrong job. Harold said he was not properly prepared for one of the specific jobs he had in the Navy, but it was due to an unusual set of circumstances. This is an example of well-intentioned training that did not produce the results anticipated. While it is a fairly unusual occurrence, these "misses" do happen. Sometimes well-intentioned efforts miss the target. Mistakes can occur in employee development in complex organizations.

> The Navy did not train me properly for the role. I was working on air control systems. They were critical systems that helped bring planes closer together to shoot at each other. My superior sent a letter requesting that I be allowed to stay on the project. Instead, I was going to be assigned to a nuclear submarine. With the submarine assignment they sent me to 5 weeks of atomic weapons school. Then, after that training, they changed my orders. I ended up on a destroyer, but I never got the training for that assignment. I should have been trained in anti-submarine warfare, but I was not. So, I was trained in atomic weapons, which I never used, and ended up overseeing an anti-submarine warfare on a destroyer, which I knew nothing about, (H.G., 2022).

Sometimes there is a disconnect between the plans for training and the outcome. There can also be a mismatch between the individual and the role. The importance of training and proper oversight of those being developed for any management or leadership role should be taken seriously in any organization.

Participant Steve said the company he worked for also had a management skill development program. The training included various modules or components for your own personal development as well as training in how to manage others. Training included things like conflict management, team building, building corporate alignment and planning. It was a two and a half year training program. In addition to the classes, the program included team retreats and opportunities for the trainees to interact informally with senior managers. "You can look at people at the level above you and find one who is similar so you begin to get a vision of how you yourself might grow in your career" (S.S. 2022). He said that those opportunities were very valuable. "Across the management team it is really helpful because you begin to see that there are people that are similar to you and that's really encouraging as a younger person or newer person. So, it gives you hope meeting these people" (S.S. 2022). In addition to the time in class, Steve said his training program also assigned a great deal of reading material throughout the program.

I asked Mark about what he is seeing in terms of current trends in leadership training. "Everybody is talking about trying to get leadership training and management training but it's lacking, and you just have no mentors out there" (M. H., 2022).

When I asked Mel about current training programs, he said leadership training is just not offered as much as it was early in his career. He said that the type of training he received is rarely offered to leadership trainees today.

> If you have a degree, experience, and credentials, they expect you to be able to come in and do the job and there is no structured training. Or they hire people to train who are not knowledgeable. Training that is basically the blind leading the blind. They let those who don't have the right knowledge train," (M.C., 2022).

If you are going to have a leadership program, it should be organized and of good quality. There should be a combination of teaching methods and variety of instructors and mentors. The skill level of those hired to conduct the training also matters. Having a training that essentially is "the blind leading the blind" as Mel describes, is worse than no training at all. Once people complete a training program, or even one class they may believe that now they are "done" having "finished' what was required of them. Regardless of the effectiveness, many organizations continue to handle training in this manner.

> It's easier, faster and it provides a way to expand a manager quickly. It's faster and cheaper to do it that way. No one has the time to go to training for 3-6 months. It's a revolving door of the untrained (leaders) trying to train new people and not having the skills necessary to train those individuals (M.C., 2022).

If organizations use internal training, they need to elevate the quality of the program as much as possible. The types of people conducting the training need to be skilled presenters. They need to be able to earn the respect of the audience. They need to be able to communicate extremely well. Leadership training also must include an experienced leader at some point during the training. The type of program that Steve described allows trainees to interact with experienced leaders and gain valuable insight just be talking to them. Any leadership training program should include excellent trainers, outside speakers with real world leadership experience, and relevant backgrounds, case studies, readings, and on the job practice.

> You have to have a leadership program that has specific goals within the training program. Individuals need to complete goals. You need to assign an experienced, qualified mentor and you need benchmarks. You also need to know if this person a good for the organization? Is this organization built for you? Some people get into leadership training and realize that's not what they want. You need to have a formal training program with people who know what they are doing (M.C., 2022).

Mel explained that part of the problem is simple economics. Businesses can no longer afford to train people thoroughly. Work culture has changed. Rather than remaining with one company throughout a person's career, we change jobs more frequently. With this change, it becomes even more costly to train. Many employers cannot invest the amount of money required to train people who are not likely to stay long-term. Now, many employers create a weak facsimile of a leadership training program and rely on that for employee growth and development. They use inexperienced internal training staff, existing and possibly unskilled leaders. They may rely on consultants or external programs through an outside vendor. That can be better than poor internal training, however, there is a possibility that external training will leave gaps in things like culture, industry, informal leadership, organizational history and organizational politics. Those topics will need to be handled internally. A possible resource for organization-specific internal training could be retirees from the organization or industry. Employees who have already separated or retired know the internal workings but may have an easier time discussing them since they no longer have to worry about their own role in the organization. Those currently in leadership roles within the organization may be reluctant to disclose political issues or discuss "sacred cows" due to their own need for self-preservation.

As Good as It Gets

Those elevated to leadership positions who are not particularly good leaders will develop people to the extent of their own skills and knowledge. Unskilled leaders will produce more of the same and the system perpetuates itself. Weak leaders also tend to hire weak people, so their weakness is not exposed. Weak leaders do not like to be challenged so they must find compliant and deferential employees. More formal training could make a significant difference in an organization already populated with a group of people in leadership roles lacking strong leadership skills.

While going through his training program, Mark said it was more than just the operational side of the business or management mechanics. They also included an on-the-job training component.

> They worked on our presentation skills and then and then there was more informal or in-house training as well. It proved very, very valuable. I felt very fortunate at that stage of my career because I was like a lot of people coming out of college. You're

used to relying on books. You're raw in terms of your skill set so I was very scared initially to just take that first step. But that information helped me so clearly. Whatever they used, it was very applicable to me. I really appreciate that now (M.H., 2022).

Mel said he also thought the on-the-job segment of his training was important. He also brought up the importance of mentors as your career progresses.

(Company name) gave me a solid foundation but I learned more from on-the-job training. I had a couple of good mentors along the way. I found out later that some people were mentoring me, and I didn't even realize it at the time. I found that the strictest bosses were the ones I learned the most from. Even though they were difficult to work for, I learned a lot from those situations. A lot of that was on the job training – learning as I was going through it (M.C., 2022).

Mel also explained the importance of knowing who you are leading. Understanding your followers can make a huge difference.

In L.A., there was a wide range of different personalities and cultures – different types of learning styles and alternative lifestyles – not just the corporate issues but understanding the people, the individuals. Knowing that with different people there are certain things you have to be sensitive to. Muslims, Asians,

Armenians – different groups, and you need to be aware of that (M.C., 2022).

When you take the time to get to know your followers, you can learn much about them along these lines. Misunderstanding can occur simply due to lack of understanding or awareness. Training for leaders working with diverse teams should include some cultural component. It is a way to connect with employees if you show respect for who they are as a person. In international companies, cultural training is typically viewed as critical for leaders working across cultural boundaries (Hofstede et al. 2010). This component to leadership training should not be reserved for international companies or for individuals managing international teams. The United States is a diverse country, and most organizations will include people from wide ranging cultural backgrounds. Cultural competency can help a leader connect and communicate better with followers.

High Potential Leader Selection

We have already discussed the shortcomings of most current training for leaders. Without real life experience, feedback, and ongoing advice and support it is very difficult for someone who has never been a leader to become one. The first step organizations should take to develop leaders is to select only those with high potential for leadership. We know leadership is based on traits so selecting someone without the personal traits of a leader makes the development process more challenging. Rather than putting people in a role who do not exhibit the traits of a leader, recruiters and those tasked with organizational development should hone the skills necessary to recognize leadership traits. The best time to determine the potential an individual has for leadership is at the time of hire or promotion. A person hired for a specific skill set may be very successful with that particular skill, but that does not mean they should be promoted to management. Those with management potential and leadership traits should be sought at the recruitment effort if that is what is desired. If you want to be sure you have good leaders, there are two ways to achieve it. Either you need to hire people who are already clearly identifiable leaders, or you need to select people with leadership potential and then be sure they are provided with an extensive training and development program.

If you think you can train leaders, you must have a highly skilled, experienced and perceptive training team capable of selecting existing employees and developing those unique skills. In addition to the quality of staff tasked with the development process, it is also critical that the existing team of leaders include at least a few people willing and able to mentor the new and future leaders. Without a long-term quality training program with progressive follow up and a mentorship process, a leadership development program will likely fail. Training programs should focus on skills and traits that may be enhanced or developed, understanding that there are limitations. If someone really wants to be in leadership then I believe the best option is to focus on what you can change and adapt to what you can't change. We can work around personality and adapt to different styles. We can learn how to communicate with an introvert, and we can build strategies around weakness. Focus on areas that can be influenced and developed such as emotional intelligence, social intelligence, and team building. Then, accept reality and be honest about the strength and capability of your leadership team.

Honest Conversations

An important component of the recruitment and selection of future leaders is to provide a forum for honest discussion and feedback. Some people will be certain that they are destined for leadership, yet the people they work with are not convinced. Rather than setting someone up for failure, difficult conversations should take place. Even employers investing heavily in leadership training may not be able to develop the leaders they desire if they begin with the wrong people and that problem is compounding if those people are not very self-aware.

People are not always the best judges of themselves. An individual convinced of his or her own leadership ability may completely misunderstand what leadership really entails. It may be that they do not see themselves realistically. Some have built false confidence that is not warranted. One complaint often heard from seasoned leaders is that entry level employees consider themselves far more competent than they really are at that moment in time. In our current culture, children are often praised and rewarded in an effort to keep all students happy.

Schools are reluctant to give anything but good grades. Teachers and coaches are fearful of offering anything but positive affirmations and compliments. Parents may inadvertently fuel this fire with ongoing praise regardless of what their child truly deserves. When students leave the "safe space" of school and comfort of home, it is understandable why they may have culture shock when they arrive at the workplace and are not immediately appreciated. A bad day on the job may be the first time a young person is on the receiving end of a difficult conversation.

When people are promoted into leadership without the necessary traits, skills, and abilities, this can cause great disruption for an organization. "Those who think they know, but are mistaken, and act upon their mistakes, are the most dangerous people to have in charge" (Thatcher, 2002, p. 104). We owe it to people to be honest about their capabilities and their potential. Reinforcing someone who is not a leader can be damaging to the people around him or her, not to mention the organization. It may be a very unpleasant conversation, but it must take place.

Trait theory has never been disproven despite many attempts to do so (Northouse, 2016). It is just politically incorrect to tell people that they were not born to be leaders. A very large, profitable, industry has been built around "creating" leaders, so a heavy emphasis on traits is not appreciated or encouraged. Many organizations ignore that reality, to their own detriment. While there may be factors in addition to traits, studies continue to identify specific personal traits that are positively associated with leadership, regardless of any training or development.

Stogdill completed two surveys in 1948 and 1974 to identify how people became leaders. He found that leaders are distinctive from other organizational players due to eight traits: intelligence, alertness, insight, responsibility, initiative, persistence, self-confidence, and sociability (Northouse, 2016). He initially thought that situational factors were more important than traits but eventually determined that both situational factors and traits were critical in determining leadership. "In essence, the second survey validated the original trait idea that a leader's characteristics are indeed a part of leadership (Northouse, 2016, p. 21). The list of traits that are positively identified with leadership, based on Stogdill's second survey, are listed below.

1. Drive for responsibility and task completion
2. Vigor and persistence in pursuit of goals
3. Risk taking and originality in problem solving
4. Drive to exercise initiative in social situations
5. Self-confidence and sense of personal identity
6. Willingness to accept consequences of decisions and actions
7. Readiness to absorb interpersonal stress
8. Willingness to tolerate frustration and delay
9. Ability to influence other people's behavior
10. Capacity to structure social interaction systems to the purpose at hand

Various studies of leadership traits and characteristics contain similarities. Some more recent studies include social intelligence and social awareness. Emotional intelligence and problem solving are also identified. According to Northouse (2016), a century of research has provided, "an extended list of traits that individuals might hope to possess or wish to cultivate if they want to be perceived as leaders" (p. 23). Central traits include intelligence, self-confidence, determination, integrity, and sociability.

If we look at these identified leadership traits, many clearly are not training topics in a corporate environment. We cannot train intelligence, for example. Integrity is also something that is more connected to character and character development that comes from parental guidance, not corporate training (Griffin, 2021). Sociability rests with personality as well. People tend to be introverted or extroverted without the ability to change from one to the other. Extroverts tend to have a much easier natural sociability than introverts.

Adapting to Reality

Organizations interested in developing and training leaders would be wise to focus on what can be improved and not have expectations that simply cannot be met. If people available for leadership roles do not seem to have the preponderance of natural traits, we have to work within those constraints. Particularly for smaller companies and non-profit organizations, it may be more challenging to attract the best quality leaders because of the competition offering better pay and benefits. Those same organizations also will be the ones less likely to afford a quality leadership training program. Perfection does not often exist in this world, so there is a reality we must adapt to. We can be honest about it, recognize what we have, identify the skills gaps, and try to shore up gaps, and be creative and astute in attracting and identifying those with the best chance for success. Like with so many things in management, an honest assessment and open discussion can be invaluable. Some people will immediately be excellent leaders. Some people just need some training and coaching and they will become very capable leaders. Some might be really good people who work hard to improve but will never be particularly good leaders. Some people may only be mediocre or worse and never get better. Some should never be leaders at all.

    One other important aspect in terms of recruiting leaders and identifying prospective leaders is the quality of your recruiter or recruitment team. Recruiting leaders is not an easy task and most internal human resources staff will have little or no experience in fielding this particular type of candidate. Organizations that do not have highly skilled internal recruiters should invest in an external recruiter or recruitment firm specializing in sourcing leaders. This is well worth the additional expense if it saves the organization from the consequences of a failed leader and all the collateral damage that goes with it.

    It's important how we select mentors for those seeking to become leaders. A leader, towards the end of their career, may find a great deal of reward in leaving a legacy of talented people to continue the work once they leave. Human resources can regularly have discussions with those in leadership roles to inquire about their interest in developing future leaders as mentors.

Participant Mel said mentoring and developing others was one of his greatest joys of leadership. He genuinely enjoyed mentoring and guiding people aspiring to advancement. "I was an effective trainer and mentor for my direct reports. I committed time to it, and I followed up. I had regular one-on-ones with my direct reports. I took it seriously. I made sure I set aside time for progress checks," (M.C., 2022). Mel said he would also ask his employees to repeat back to him what he had said to check for understanding. He made sure his direct reports were understanding to the extent that they could paraphrase what he had told them.

Mel also followed a "seek first to understand" approach. He listened to his team to be sure he knew exactly what they were learning and what they were not learning. "I would come back to them and ask them, 'what could you have done differently' or 'tell me what went well and what did not' and I did a lot of pre-positioning before they met with an employee or management. We would practice or role play. Afterwards, I would follow up and ask them, 'what did you learn?' (M.C., 2022). Mel emphasized that mentoring requires a major time commitment. It is not something that can be done easily or quickly. Mentoring staff is something higher level leaders will need to make time for if they want to develop their staff. In Mel's (2022) words, "It is about committing the time, being sincere, and following up and finding out what worked and what didn't work."

Steve said that he was involved in training people on an individual basis. One of the techniques he used was to just start assigning projects to someone who wanted opportunities to grow. He described a situation where he assisted a younger person in her development and how it helped advance her career and how much she appreciated it. We will use the pseudonym "Ann" as we share his comments. "At my retirement, 'Ann' was there. She's now well established in her career. She thanked me for those early steps that I took to support her career" (S.S. 2022).

Another opportunity Steve found for reaching staff was just to eat lunch with them on a regular basis. The same group of people would meet and have the opportunity, in an informal environment, to ask questions or discuss ideas. "We did it routinely for a couple of years. It was just a place for them to talk about projects and things they had questions about. We would have those conversations during lunch and those were really helpful" (S.S. 2022). He said they would ask questions about things he may have already experienced such as challenges with motivating staff. He had the opportunity during these informal lunch gatherings to share his years of experience with newer managers.

Often a more senior manager is pleased to be able to share his or her experience and knowledge and find it rewarding. It's nice to know that all that experience can be utilized beyond the tenure of one individual. The company can retain more of its organizational expertise by passing along experience from older leaders to the young ones coming up. In addition to the value to the organization, there is personal fulfilment in knowing you have had an impact on another person's life. Steve described his mentoring of others as something he found both fulfilling and fun. He said he followed their careers and continued looking out for them over the years. He would check in to see how they were doing, and would continue helping them at different career junctions.

> 'Ann' came to my retirement celebration and just gave me a big hug. It was really special. Other senior people at the event actually commented on how I had mentored them in other ways by just be being courageous, standing up against senior management at times, and just being courageous enough to stand up for somebody else and give them an opportunity. Sometimes you just have to do it. You have to be courageous. (S.S. 2022)

The benefits of mentorship exist for both participants. Some younger people are dismissive of older leaders but to do so is a loss. Seasoned leaders have a wealth of knowledge and have lived a lifetime of lessons that could be invaluable to someone with few years of experience under their belt.

Making Mistakes

Reputation is difficult to earn but easy to destroy. One bad leader can destroy years of hard-earned respect within an organization. An overly dictatorial leader can impact the career of trajectory his or her team members. An unskilled leader relying on intimidation to control employees costs the organization the potential contribution of staff and may cost them the employee entirely. Hiring or promoting a person to leadership who should not be in a leadership role can cause enormous damage to individuals and the organization. Status quo can be less detrimental than a leader lacking in intelligence, integrity, and other traits necessary for success. The damage may reverberate well beyond that individual with a domino effect that can hurt the organization for years.

While people may not be easily able to describe a good leader, they certainly recognize a bad one. When people feel threatened or intimidated, they either stay in the job and become a shadow, hiding in self-protection mode, or they leave looking for a better environment.

The worst leader I experienced in my career was someone who was so clearly not a leader that he even questioned the wisdom of those who put him in that position. He knew he was not cut out for leadership, yet it was a role that was given to him, so he accepted the position with the corresponding high salary. While he was a very nice person and may have been a decent employee in other roles, he was definitely not successful in the role he was performing, and it was evident to those who reported to him. A leadership role exposed his weaknesses, rather than highlighting his strengths.

It is difficult to turn down a promotion or higher-level role when you are asked to take one. It's a compliment and it's exciting so people tend to jump to accept a higher level role when offered. It takes humility, honesty and selflessness to turn down a higher-level position. Those who know what is best for them, and the organization, will make the decision to reject an offer, even if there are personal advantages to it. I have seen people reject promotions and offers of management positions because they knew it would not be the best use of their skills, or they knew they would not like it. Some chose not to accept a leadership role because they knew it would not be best for the organization.

For example, I worked with a woman who was frequently encouraged to apply for a management role. She had been with the organization for many years and functioned exceptionally well in her job. She was highly competent and responsible. She was universally liked and appreciated. Multiple managers tried to recruit her for a management role. Each time she refused. Rather than seeking advancement to a management position, she recognized that she was best served, and the organization was best served, if she stayed in her current job. She also knew she would not like management. She stayed in that same role until her retirement.

Another young man I had the opportunity to work with responded similarly when asked to take a management role. He initially accepted the position, started and job, and worked at it the best he could. He quickly realized, however, that he did not want a management role. Rather than muddle through, as most would do, he went to human resources and asked to be moved back to an individual contributor role. Making this change meant a reduction in salary, yet he knew it was the right decision for him. He did not want to disappoint his team or himself. He had the humility and integrity to reject a role that was not the best fit for his traits and skills.

Young leaders, or those aspiring to leadership, would be well advised to take time to talk to more seasoned leaders. Don't be afraid to seek advice from someone more experienced. Even if there is no formal mentorship program, there may be skilled and seasoned leaders willing and able to at least take the time to provide the benefit of their years of experience to younger employees.

If you are a seasoned leader, you can assist in developing the next generation of leaders by showing interest in their progress, asking questions about their projects, and offering assistance. Sometimes, it's just being willing to listen. Having a conversation, offering advice and being a sounding board can be beneficial. Particularly as fewer companies invest in the kinds of training programs that would really be impactful, people need to find their own opportunities to grow, develop, and advance. It may require self-directed training and initiative to be properly positioned to advance.

As we have hopefully effectively described in this chapter, leadership training is not a one-and-done project. It is a long-term commitment with investments from both the individual and the organization. Anyone seriously interested in a leadership role should be prepared to be a life-long learner, open to constructive criticism, correction, and honest feedback. It may be more of a challenge than originally considered, but if you decide to pursue a leadership role, you will find the position much more satisfying if you know you achieved the role with the best of intentions. If you decide leadership is not the best path, there are many ways to contribute and accomplish great things.

Whatever you do, it's important that you know you applied yourself, had positive impact, and demonstrated ethical behavior to those around you. At the end of your career, you will be able to look back with contentment and gratification.

CHAPTER NINE
SUCCESSFULLY NAVIGATING THE LANDSCAPE

A recent study conducted by the organizational consulting firm, Korn Ferry, identified some changes in desired leadership traits and skills post-pandemic. The Korn Ferry study looked at more than 20,500 psychometric assessments of CEOs and others in leadership positions at 674 of the 846 large, publicly traded companies included in the Drucker Institute rankings of the best managed companies (Thomas, 2021). They emphasized traits, again, emphasizing the foundational aspects of the individual. "Traits are personality characteristics central to who a person is. Competencies are observable skills that come naturally to some but can also be attained and honed with experience" (Wartzman & Tang, 2022).

The study showed that participants were even more interested than in the past in the leader's ability to adapt and lead through difficult and challenging environments (Wartzman & Tang, 2022). A similar study two years ago also resulted in the same top trait listed as the that identified in the newer study. The top trait is the "tolerance for ambiguity". Earlier studies, prior to the pandemic, considered the most critically important things to be team building, engaging employees, effective communication and cultivating innovation. This represents a significant change. After many years of being told to work on employee engagement and team building, the top-rated companies and top leaders in those companies no longer consider those to be of great value. All have dropped lower in desirability.

The new study indicates that, in addition to "tolerance for ambiguity", the four new competencies now rated in the top five are "global perspective," "manages ambiguity," "interpersonal savvy" and "instills trust." One theory is that the change in most desirable traits is directly related to the pandemic. Those who successfully led their organizations through the pandemic were required to have a more global understanding and awareness. During this time, change was constant, so leaders were forced to react quickly with a great deal of unknowns. They often did not have all the information they would have liked to have to make a good decision, but they had to make decisions regardless. They had to use good judgment and display confidence in the face of a great deal of fear. The touchy-feely days of team building, and employee engagement gave way to the critical decision-making of a leader faced with a global emergency. Followers needed to know that leaders considered their health and wellbeing. They needed to have sensitivity to medical situations and family issues. Decisions may have required imagination, creativity, and adaptability when faced with ill employees, customer abandonment, supply chain disruptions, vendor and partner failures, and a wide range of other distractions and interferences. True leaders emerged while others cowered, deflected, and hid behind government bureaucracy.

Now that we have covered these topics, how can you move forward? There are several aspects and individuals participating in the land of leadership who engage in these issues from a different perspective. Whether you are currently a leader or follower, someone aspiring to grow, or those recruiting and nurturing individuals through the employment life cycle, you have a role to play in the leadership landscape.

Summing Up: Individual Leaders

As individuals, we must take responsibility for ourselves, our careers, and our path in life. If you are choosing leadership, first, really be self-aware and give yourself an honest assessment. Ask yourself if you really do have the traits of a leader. Ask yourself if you are really willing to put in the time and energy to continue to develop yourself and be a lifelong learner. Recognize that if you have few traits of a leader, you will have to work harder on training and development than someone who has inborn traits.

The need for leadership is great. Not everyone can be Winston Churchill or George Washington. The rest of us do the best we can. Our obligation is to be aware of our strengths and weaknesses and manage our employees and our assignments with those two things in mind. We should be constantly looking for opportunities to improve ourselves through reading, attending training, and seeking mentors. We should surround ourselves with smart people who work hard to be good leaders and effective decision-makers.

As you are leading people, remember that humans are complicated and messy. Give yourself the freedom to make mistakes and give your followers the same. The important thing is the attitude in the face of a mistake. Are we willing to accept constructive criticism and listen to wiser voices or are we going to blame others, argue, and be defensive? Don't be afraid to offer constructive criticism to those who report to you and know that, although it is uncomfortable, it is necessary to help them to improve. Even if there is conflict, communication is necessary and valuable. Even if there is disagreement, this is time to come to an understanding. A subordinate unwilling to accept direction or correction is not someone that will function well on a team. Leaders should recognize that those determined to do things their own way will be difficult followers to manage.

Decision making is a critical function of leadership. It should not be taken lightly. Decisions should not come from emotion or a knee-jerk reaction. Decisions should be thoughtful and given an appropriate amount of time relevant to the complexity, level of risk, number of stakeholders, and potential consequences of outcomes (Griffin-Ray, 2022). An indecisive leader is not a leader. A culture of non-decision is an unattractive environment for nearly all participants (Griffin-Ray, 2022).

Finally, remember that it can be lonely at the top. There is a great deal of stress in a leadership role, and the weight of significant decisions can be a burden. Leaders need to be sure to relax the mind and refresh the spirit on a regular basis. Personal relationships can make a bad day better and turn a good day into a celebration. It's important to nurture personal relationships, a healthy lifestyle, and mental and spiritual well-being. We should not let the job overtake every aspect of our life. It's been said often but always bears repeating. No one wishes for more time at work when they are on their death bed. Personal relationships, often neglected, mean so much more than we realize in the midst of our chaotic careers. It is when we slow down and take time to think and reflect that we realize how very precious people in our lives are. It's important to remember that our families and friends also need our time and attention. Make it a life-long goal to become a great leader, but don't forget to be a good person.

A leader also needs good followers. Recognize that some people are just not going to be good for your team and will not help you become a successful leader. Followers have a role to play critical to the success of the leader. Followers that are troublemakers will always be a problem. Recognize the problem and remove it.

Followers

Followers should start by recognizing that the role of follower is distinct and valuable. While you may be seeking to become a leader, you cannot neglect your role as follower. Supporting your direct report is your responsibility. You do not have to like that person, but it is the obligation of a follower to follow and be diligent and reliable when implementing directives that come from above. Clearly there are exceptions when it comes to an illegal or immoral directive, but otherwise, following directions should be an expectation. Organizations can only function effectively if each player in the organizational hierarchy fulfills his or her role.

For those followers seeking leadership, you must assess your current situation to determine if there is an opportunity to grow into the role or roles you desire. There can be many barriers to promotional opportunities. It could be as simple as there are no openings in higher level roles, particularly in a smaller organization. While many people have looked for advancement opportunities, sometimes there simply are not any available. That means when you are ready to be promoted you need to understand the availability and the timeline for any potential opening and if nothing suits your timeline, it may be time to seek employment elsewhere. You may need to look for the role you want in a new organization.

If there are roles you believe you could fulfill and yet are not given the opportunity, it could be that there is a cultural mismatch between you and the organization. Often referred to as the "fit factor" a skilled and talented person may simply not be a fit for that particular department or organization. A manager may be concerned about the team and looking for a person who can fill a role within a team. Factors unrelated to skill and ability can weigh in on a promotional decision when a department needs to function as a team.

If you want to be promoted, but are not being offered a promotion, it could be that the role you are currently in is considered critical and your ability to fill it is highly valued. Many people are incredible individual contributors and if you add the burden of employee management it dilutes the individual contributions. Much of management includes administrative tasks like time sheet review and approval, scheduling, and basic organizational activities. It involves listening to employees when they have conflicts or personal issues. Management activities can take up a great deal of time.

It could be that perhaps leadership is not the right path to follow, as previously discussed. Not everyone is cut out to be a manager or leader.

Someone may be hindering your promotion intentionally to benefit themselves. It could be that a more senior leader does not want the competition that you might present.

It could be that there is some favoritism allowing less qualified or less skilled people to be advanced while others languish. Managers typically hire people that they like or can relate to. Each layer in the organizational structure is subject to subjective opinions, which can result in biased hiring and promoting. It is a reality of corporate life and, other than discriminatory practices, cannot be completely eliminated.

Before becoming a frustrated follower, it's important to assess the political landscape. What is the opportunity? If there is favoritism, be aware that your own contributions may never be appreciated and your abilities may be ignored. Understanding the political landscape of your organization would be very helpful. For example, does your department seem to have political clout? Does your department frequently get approval for requests? Do you have adequate personnel or are you constantly asking for new employees? When you ask, are you rejected?

How does senior leadership treat you or your manager? Do you see your manager going to lunch with the CEO? Is your manager part of the "in crowd" or does he or she seem to work more as an individual? These things will impact how you are seen, at whatever level of followership you exist, and it will tell you what the likely landscape is for your climb up the ladder.

If you are not getting promoted or have never had anyone ask you about your interest in promotional opportunities, it may be time for a direct conversation with the person you report to. If you have never been given feedback along these lines, you can ask questions and request some guidance on how you could better prepare for a higher level role or a leadership development opportunity. You can consider asking your leader, or another leader in the organization if he or she would consider mentoring you. You should be aware of what kind of training exists within your organization and how it is viewed by current leaders. Ask those who have been through the training. Did they find it valuable? Did it result in a promotion to leadership? If your organization does not offer leadership training, that is something to consider in terms of your career path. The opportunity a promotion, particularly into management or leadership, may never materialize if the organization has no ability or interest in providing a career development program.

If you recognize that the problem within the leadership landscape is not your lack of ability, but the lack of opportunity within the organization, it may be time to seek another organization. Dr. Henry Cloud (2010) suggests that people should be aware of the difference between what is worth fixing and what should simply come to an end. "To hold onto hope when what you really have is merely a wish is to fail to grasp reality" (Cloud, 2010, p. 91). He says that the past is the best predictor of the future. How have you been treated by your manager and the organization? Have you been approached and offered career development or training? Has your manager talked to you about promotional opportunities? Has she or she asked you about your career goals? If you have not been promoted in the past, how long do you hold onto hope that at some point something will change to result in the promotion? What is going to change to make those in power see you differently than they have in the past?

It may be that the person or persons that have the power to promote you simply will not do it for his or her own reasons. Cloud (2010) says it is important to remember who holds power and not just be focused on what you wish will happen. There may be people with power that do not want to see you get promoted. You have to recognize these facts, as displeasing as they may be. It may be time to accept that the only way to get where you want in your career is to find another organization. There may be nothing wrong with you and nothing wrong with your current organization. It's simply that there is a barrier that you cannot overcome if you remain in your current organization. It is possible to leave a job on a positive note. It may be time for a change. "Your brain's hard wiring can resist change, as we have seen. But, at the same time, you know you must change if you are going to end the misery of the present and get to the future that you desire" (Cloud, 2010, p. 149).

Change is difficult, but it also can result in finding the right environment and culture where you can shine. Before accepting that you are stuck in a role regardless of your desires, consider looking for a more suitable situation and organization to achieve your goals. "Your next step always depends on two ingredients: how well you are maximizing where you are right now and how ready you are to do what is necessary to get to the next place. And sometimes that depends on ending some of what is happening today" (Cloud, 2011, p. 230). It is difficult to leave a job when it creates uncertainty, anxiety, and fear. That is why so many people stay at a job where they are frustrated, rather than seeking something that would offer better opportunities. Cloud says if you really want a better tomorrow, "some parts of today may have to come to a necessary ending" (Cloud, 2011, p. 230).

Human Resources and Training

Those tasked with the human resources and/or training responsibilities of an organization have a critical role to play in the leadership landscape. As explained in earlier chapters, having a quality leadership training program can have an impact in the success of developing new leaders. Human resources staff can take the lead and offer another display of their value in this capacity. Human resources leaders can champion training and development programs for staff.

If you are in a human resources or training role, consider proposing a leadership training program if your organization does not have one. There are plenty of resources and ways to outsource training if you do not have the experienced staff to manage a program internally. The key is to get quality resources and reputable training. If you are in a small company, a training program may not be possible, but you can still have impact by creating on-the-job training opportunities and partnering potential leaders with excellent senior leaders. Even if you only find one senior leader willing and able to mentor, that person can mentor two or three people. Already you have multiplied your impact in the leadership capacity of the organization. It may not be the perfect scenario, but your efforts can still have impact.

Recognizing talent is a talent. Human resources leaders should hone their skills, or partner with someone known for the ability to recognize potential leaders. The benefit to the organization is great if the human resources professional(s) can add value to the effort by recruiting talented leaders or those with potential for leadership. The best place to stop bad leadership is at the front door. If you can be skilled enough to deflect a bad leader while attracting and hiring good leaders, the development requirements are less daunting.

Senior Executive/CEO

One of the biggest pitfalls of the senior leader is when accidentally or intentionally they are surrounded with sycophants. Everyone likes to be liked and to feel comfortable. Many leaders will default to what is comfortable, rather than to what is challenging. A talented leadership team can be invaluable to a senior executive, but they can also be detrimental. When the leadership team only placates the top executive(s) they are doing a disservice to the executive and to the organization. A good leader should welcome constructive criticism, honest feedback, and open debate.

Senior leaders fearful of conflict or challenge should not be in a senior leadership role. It costs the organization in many significant ways. Those within the various levels of the organization may feel discouraged when they can tell that the top-level leaders do not want to hear any other opinions or opposing viewpoints. Employees who care about the organization and who want to contribute their skills and talents will eventually leave to seek opportunities where they feel valued and where their voices will be heard. Those who stay will be the ones with little other choice, or without the confidence or character to make a difference in the organization. They will do nothing to jeopardize their own security and comfort. They simply go along to get along rendering themselves mediocre at best.

If you are a senior leader, do not reject those who challenge you. A CEO should be challenged by others and questioned, and a diversity of opinions should be encouraged. A confident leader will appreciate honest input and truthful answers. If a leader functions in an echo chamber, the organization is more likely to have problems that should have been foreseen. If there is no one on the team with the courage to confront a senior leader on what may be a bad idea, it places the senior leader in a weaker and more vulnerable position. If you want to ensure your continued success as a senior leader, surround yourself with those who have the intelligence, commitment, and courage to tell you when you are wrong and why they think so, professionally and respectfully. Every senior leader should want those reporting to him or be honest and upfront, even when it's uncomfortable.

Conclusion

There are multiple players involved in the leadership landscape. Organizations genuinely interested in building a pipeline of leaders will need to invest heavily with all the processes and with all the people with a role to play. Individuals must also take responsibility for their own development, advancement, or they need to develop a plan for exit. An individual who takes responsibility for themselves will be far more likely to achieve a fulfilling career. Honest conversations, direct requests, and self-awareness are critical tools for those looking to grow in their careers and become leaders. If you are determined to become part of the leadership landscape, then you may have to forge your own path to get there. In the end, the path you forge may just be the best possible route you could have taken with the results even exceeding your expectation.

APPENDIX A

A brief description of each participant is provided.

Participant: Mark Hoaglin

Mark has over 30 years of leadership experience in banks, credit unions, and broker/dealers. He has managed large national sales divisions and was a CEO for a California-based broker/dealer. Mark holds a bachelor's degree from Stanford University, a Master of Business Administration (MBA) from the University of San Diego. He has also earned the CFP designation. Mark has a long history of athletics, playing multiple sports. He earned a scholarship to play football at Stanford University.

Participant: Steve Schlahta

Steve was the Research Chief Operating Officer for the Earth & Biological and Physical and Computational Sciences Directorates for several years providing overall leadership for the operational stewardship and programmatic execution functions across five research divisions and two project management offices. Prior to his Research Chief Operating Officer role, Steve was the Nuclear Science and Legacy Waste (NSLW) Project Management Office Director. Steve has an extensive history of managing complex and multi-disciplinary projects. His experience includes U.S. Department of Energy (DOE) carbon management and nuclear waste clean-up challenges, microchannel chemical processing and thermal management systems, and advanced characterization techniques. Steve earned a Bachelor of Arts degree in Economics from California State University, San Bernardino. He was an Honors Graduate, Phi Kappa Phi.

Participant: Harold Griffin

Harold has over 35 years of experience in management within large, well-known, corporations. He led several service divisions and sales groups. He began his career in a management role as an officer in the U.S. Navy. Harold holds a Bachelor of Arts degree with an economics major from Holy Cross College, graduating cum laude. He also earned a Master of Business Administration (M.B.A.) from Northwestern University.

Participant: Mel Calloway

Mel has over 45 years of experience in banking. He created a sales and service culture in several organizations leading sales and service teams, mentoring hundreds of people during his career. Mel earned a Bachelor of Science degree in economics with a minor in political science from N. Carolina A & T State University. He is also a certified trainer for Oz Principals and Cohen and Brown. He earned a management certificate for banking at the University of Southern California.

Power, Politics, and the Leadership Landscape

REFERENCES

Adjibolosoo, S. (2005). The Human Factor in Leadership Effectiveness, Tate Publishing, Mustang, OK.

Adjibolosoo, S. (2018). The Human Factor Approach to Managerial and Organizational Efficiency and Effectiveness, Palgrave MacMillan, Cham, Switzerland.

Aristotle, Nicomachean Ethics, (1985), Hacket Publishing, Indianapolis, IN

Axelrod, R., & Cohen, M.d. (2000). Harnessing Complexity: Organizational implications of a science frontier. Basic Books, New York, NY.

Byrne, D., & Callaghan, G. (2014). Complexity Theory and the Social Sciences. Routledge, New York, NY.

Boudreaux, D. (2022). The CEO, The American Institute for Economic Research, Great Barrington, MA.

Brookehiser, R. (2022). Twenty Years Later, A view of, and from, September 11. National Review Magazine, September 13, 2021.

Caza, A. & Jackson, B., Authentic Leadership, In Bryman, Alan, Collinson, David, K. Grint, B. Jackson & M. Uhl-Bien (Eds.), The Sage Handbook of Leadership (pp. 195-200). Thousand Oaks, CA: Sage Publications.

Chandler, J.L.S. & Kirsch, R.E. (2018). Critical Leadership Theory. Palgrave Macmillan, Basingstolke, Hampshire.

Cloud, H. (2010). Necessary Endings, The Employees, Businesses, and Relationships That All of Us Have to Give Up In order to Move Forward, Harper Collins, New York, NY.

Day, D. (2011). Leadership Development, In Bryman, Alan, Collinson, David, K. Grint, B. Jackson & M. Uhl-Bien (Eds.), The Sage Handbook of Leadership (pp. 37-48). Thousand Oaks, CA: Sage Publications.

Day. D. (2009). Executive selection is a process not a decision. Industrial and Organizational Psychology: Perspectives on Science and Practice, 2, 159-162.

Day, D. (2000). Leadership Development: A Review in Context; The Leadership Quarterly, 11-581-613.

Dean, M. (2009). Three conceptions of the relationship between power and liberty In Clegg, Stewart and Haugaard, Mark (Ed.), The Sage handbook of Power (pp. 177-191). Sage Publications Thousand Oaks, CA.

Ferch, S. R. (2012). Forgiveness and Power in the Age of Atrocity. Lanham, MD. Lexington Books.

Flatten, M. (2017), Protection Racket, Occupational Licensing Laws and the Right to Earn a Living, Goldwater Institute, Phoenix, AZ.

Fillmore, S. (2022) Research and Commentary: Washington State Proposes Commonsense Restrictions to Unilateral Gubernatorial Power During States Of Emergency, The Heartland Institute, Arlington Heights, IL. Retrieved from: https://www.heartland.org/publications-resources/publications/research--commentary-washington-state-proposes-commonsense-restrictions-to-unilateral-gubernatorial-power-during-states-of-emergency.

Follett, M. (2016). The New State, Group Organization the Solution of Popular Government, Martino Publishing, Mansfield Center, CT.

Foucault, M. (1982). The subject and power. Critical Inquiry, 8(4), 777-795.

Frankl, V. E. (1969). The Will to Meaning; Foundations and Applications of Logotherapy, New York, NY, Penguin Group.

Frankl, V. E. (2006). Man's search for meaning (4. ed. ed.). Boston, Mass: Beacon Press.

Frankl, V. E. 1. (2000). Man's search for ultimate meaning. United States: Persus Books.

French, J. R. P. Jr., & Raven, B. (1959). The bases of social power. In D.P. Cartwright, ed., Studies in social power (pp. 150-167). Ann Arbor, MI: University of Michigan, Institute for Social Research.

George, B. (2003). Authentic leadership: Rediscovering the secrets to creating lasting value Jossey-Bass, San Francisco, CA.

Giovannoni, F., & Seidmann, D. (2014). Corruption and power in democracies. Social Choice And Welfare, 42(3), 707-734. 10.1007/s00355-013-0739-x Retrieved from http://proxy.foley.gonzaga.edu/login?url=http://search.ebscohost.com.proxy.foley.gonzaga.edu/login.aspx?direct=true&db=a9h&AN=94886307&site=ehost-live

Gohler, G. (2009). Power to and Power over, in Clegg, Stewart and Haugarard, Mark, The Sage Handbook of Power (p. 27-39). Thousand Oaks, CA, Sage Publoications.

Gordon, R. (2011). Leadership and Power, in Bryman, Alan, Collinson, David, K. Grint, B.Jackson & M. Uhl-Bien (Eds.), The Sage Handbook of Leadership (pp. 195-200). Thousand Oaks, CA: Sage Publications.

Gordon, R. (2009). Power and legitimacy; From Weber to Contemporary Theory. In Clegg, Stewart and Haugaard, Mark (Ed.), Sage handbook of power (pp. 256-273).Thousand Oaks CA: Sage Publications.

Griffin-Ray, E. (2022). Decisions and Non-Decisions, A Pragmatic View of Power, Structure, and Culture in Complex Organizations, Outskirts Press, U.S.

Haight, J. (2006). The Happiness Hypothesis, Finding Modern Truth in Ancient Wisdom, Basic Books, NY

Hartley, J. & Benington, J. (2011). Political Leadership in Bryman, A. et al, Editors, Sage Handbook of Leadership, p. 203-212, Sage Publications, London, New Delhi, Los Angeles, Singapore, Washington, D.C.

Hayek. F.A. (2007). The Road to Serfdom, The University of Chicago Press, Chicago, IL

Heifetz, R. (1994). Leadership Without Easy Answers, Harvard University Press, Cambridge, MA.

Hofsteded, G., Hofsteded, G., Minkov, M. (2010). Cultures and Organizations, Intercultural Cooperation and Its Importance for Survival, McGraw Hill, New York NY.

Jaeger, J. (2021). Top Ethics and Compliance Failures of 2021, Compliance Week, 12/7/21, Retrieved from https://www.complianceweek.com/opinion/top-ethics-and-compliance-failures-of-2021/31120.article.

Jessop, B. (2009). The State and Power In Clegg, Stewart and Haugaard, Mark (Ed.), The Sage handbook of Power (pp. 367-381). Thousand Oaks, CA: Sage Publications.

Johnston, M. (2013). More than necessary, less than sufficient: Democratization and the control of corruption. Social Research, 80(4), 1237-1258. Retrieved from http:// proxy foley.gonzaga.edu/login.aspx?direct=true&db=a9h&AN=9407439&site=ehost-live.

Kets de Vries, M. & Balazs, K. (2011). The Shadow Side of Leadership, In Bryman, Alan, Collinson, David, K. Grint, B.Jackson & M. Uhl-Bien (Eds.), The Sage Handbook of Leadership (pp. 380-391). Sage Publications. Thousand Oaks, CA.

Koslowsky, M., Schwarzwald, J. (2009). Power Tactics Preference in Organizations in Tjsovold &Wisse,(Ed.s), Power and Interdependence in Organizations, Cambridge: Cambridge University Press.

Lord, R.G. & Hall, R.J. (2005). Identity, deep structure, and the development of leadership skill. The Leadership Quarterly, 16, 591-615.

Martins, N. O. (2018). An ontology of power and leadership. Journal for the Theory of Social Behavior, 48(1), 83-97.

McGrath, R. (2019). Seeing Around Corners: How to Spot Inflection Points in Business Before they Happen, Harper Collins Publishers, New York, NY.

Navot, D. (2016). Real politics and the concept of political corruption. Political Studies Review,14(4), 544-554. 10.1111/1478-9302.12079 Retrieved fromhttp://proxy.foley.gonzaga.edu/login?url=http://search.ebscohost.com.proxy.foley Gonzaga.edu/login.aspx?direct=true&db=a9hAN-119242573&site=ehost-live

Nesler, M. S., Quigley, B. M., Tedeschi, J. T., & Aguinis, H. (1994). Perceptions of power: A cognitive perspective. Social Behavior & Personality: An

International Journal, 22(4), 377-384. Retrieved from http://proxy.foley.gonzaga.edu/login?url=foley.gonzaga.edu/login.aspx?direct=true&db=a9h&AN=12807267&site=ehost-live

Northouse, P. (2016). Leadership, Theory and Practice, Sage Publications, Los Angeles, CA.

Pierro, A., Cicero, L., & Raven, B. H. (2008). Motivated compliance with bases of social power. Journal of Applied Social Psychology, 38(7), 1921-1944. 10.1111/j.1559-1816.2008.00374.x Retrieved from http://proxy.foley.gonzaga.edu/login?url=http://

search.ebscohost.com.proxy.foley.gonzaga.edu/login.aspx?direct=true&db=a9h&AN=32642842&site=ehost-live.

Rahim, M. (2009). Bases of Leader Power and Effectiveness, in Tjsvold & Wisse (eds), Power and Interdependence in Organizations, Cambridge Press, Cambridge, UK.

Raven, B. H. (2008). The bases of power and the power/interaction model of interpersonal influence. Analyses of Social Issues & Public Policy, 8(1), 1-22. 10.1111/j.1530-2415.2008.00159.x Retrieved from http://proxy.foley.gonzaga.edu/login?url=http://search.ebscohost.com.proxy.foley.gonzaga.edu/login.aspx?direct=true&db=a9h&AN=35393866&site=ehost-live.

Schatz, T. (2015). The IRS's Abuse of Power, The Hill, retrieved from http://thehill.com/blogs/pundits-blog/the-administration/254781-the-irss-abuse-of-power.

Schein, E. (2017). Organizational Culture and Leadership, Wiley Publications, Hoboken, NJ.

Securities and Exchange Commission Press Release, 9/23/2021, Retrieved fromhttps://www.sec.gov/news/press-release/2021-174.

Sen, A (2009). The Idea of Justice, Belknap Press, Harvard University Press, Cambridge, MA

Slack, E., & Estes, E. (2018). Nothing Short of Horrifying, Veteran's Groups Demand Fixes at VA Nursing Homes, USA Today, retrieved from https://www.usatoday.com/story/news/politics/2018/11/19/va-nursing-homes-veteran-groups-want-fixes-after-horrifying-reports-trump-administration-congress/2018781002/.

Smith, A. (1976). The Theory of Moral Sentiments, Liberty Fund Inc., Indianapolis, IN.

Thatcher, M. (2002). Statecraft, Strategies for a Changing World, Harper-Collins, New York, NY.

Thomas, P. (2021). The Best Managed Companies of 2021 – and How They Made it to the Top Wall Street Journal, 12/11/21, Retrieved from https://www.wsj.com/articles/best-managed-companies-2021-how-they-made-it-to-the-top-11639168146?mod=ig_managementtop250december2021.

Tjosvole, D. & Wisse, B. (2009). Power and Interdependence in Organizations, Cambridge University Press, Cambridge, U.K.

Torfing, J. (2009), Power and Discourse: Towards an Anti-Foundationalist Concept of Power, In Clegg, Stewart and Haugaard, Mark (Ed.), The Sage handbook of Power (pp. 367-381). Thousand Oaks, CA: Sage Publications.

Uhl-Bien, M. & Marion, R. (2011) Complexity Leadership Theory, In Bryman, Alan, Collinson, David, K. Grint, B.Jackson & M. Uhl-Bien (Eds.), The Sage Handbook of Leadership (pp. 468 - 477). Sage Publications. Thousand Oaks, CA.

Wang, F., & Sun, X. (2016). Absolute power leads to absolute corruption? impact of power on corruption depending on the concepts of power one holds. European Journal of Social Psychology, 46(1), 77-89. 10.1002/ejsp.2134 Retrieved from http://proxy.foley.gonzaga.edu/login?url=http://search.ebscohost.com.proxy.foley.gonzaga.edu/login.aspx?direct=true&db=a9h&AN=114639621&site=ehost-live.

Wartzman, R., & Tang, K. (2022). What Good Leadership Looks Like Now vs. Pre-Covid, The Wall Street Journal, September 17, 2022. Retrieved from What Good Leadership Looks Like Now vs. Pre-Covid – WSJ.

Walumbwa, F.O., Avolio, B.J., Gardner, W.L. Wernsing, T.S., and Peterson, S.J. (2008). Authentic leadership development and validation of a theory-based measure. Journal of Management, 34(1), 89-126.

Welch, J. (2005). Winning, Harper Collins Publishing, New York, NY.

Westwood, S. (2016). Nine Major Veteran's Affairs Failures, Washington Examiner, 8/8/2016 Retrieved from https://www.washingtonexaminer.com/nine-major-veterans-affairs- failures.

Williams, P. (2010). The Leadership Wisdom of Solomon, 28 Essential Strategies for Leading with Integrity, Standard Publishing Company, Cincinnati OH.

Wooden, J. and Carty, J. (2005). Coach Wooden's Pyramid of Success, Building Blocks for a Better Life, Revell, Grand Rapids, MI.

Yukl, G. (2009). Power and the Interpersonal Influence of Leaders. In Tjosvold, D. & Wisse, B. (Eds.), Power and Interdependence in Organizations, (p. 207-223), Cambridge, UK: Cambridge University Press.

Power, Politics, and the Leadership Landscape

www.ingramcontent.com/pod-product-compliance
Lightning Source LLC
Chambersburg PA
CBHW071401210526
45465CB00001B/192